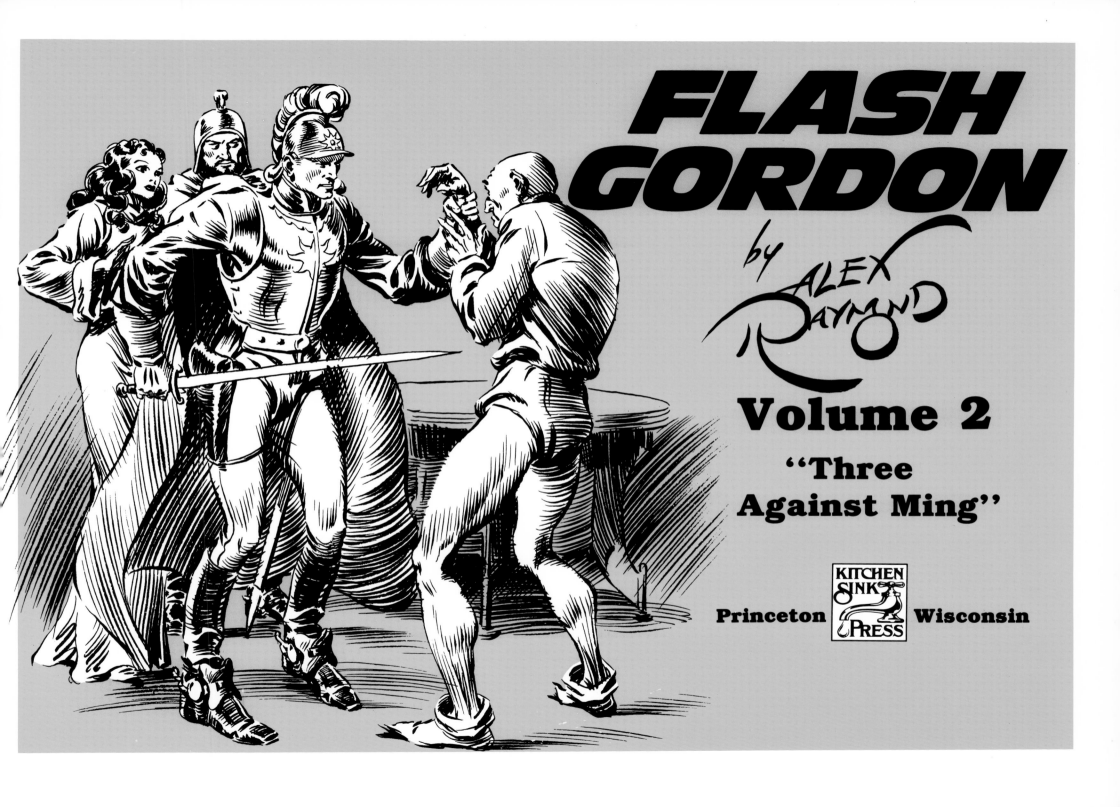

# FLASH GORDON

*by* ALEX RAYMOND

## Volume 2

### "Three Against Ming"

KITCHEN SINK PRESS

Princeton                    Wisconsin

*Flash Gordon, Volume Two: "Three Against Ming,"* is published by Kitchen Sink Press, Inc., No. 2 Swamp Rd., Princeton WI 54968. Flash Gordon pages copyright © 1935, 1936, 1937, 1990 by King Features Syndicate, Inc. Entire contents copyright © 1990 by Kitchen Sink Press, Inc. All rights reserved. Printed in Hong Kong.

**ISBN 0-87816-120-1**

Peter Poplaski, editor and cover design; Dave Schreiner, editor-in-chief; James Kitchen, production coordinator; Doreen Riley, proofreader; Denis Kitchen, publisher.

The publisher wishes to acknowledge Al Williamson, Bill Blackbeard of the San Francisco Academy of Comic Art and Richard Halegua, of Comic Art & Graffix Gallery, Cincinnati, for allowing Kitchen Sink Press to use *Flash Gordon* pages from their collections. Their generosity made this book possible.

**Library of Congress Cataloging-in-Publication Data**

Raymond, Alex, 1909-1956
    Flash Gordon / by Alex Raymond
    Contents: v. 2. Three against Ming.
    ISBN 0-87816-120-1 (v. 2) ($34.95)
    I. Title
    PN6728.F55R37    1990
    741.5'973—dc20                         90-5049
                                          CIP
        ISBN 0-87816-114-7 (v. 1)
        ISBN 0-87816-120-1 (v. 2)

This is the second volume in a six volume set reprinting the entire run of Alex Raymond's *Flash Gordon*. Kitchen Sink Press publishes a full line of books, comics, art prints, and other comics-related material, including Al Capp's *Li'l Abner*, Milton Caniff's *Steve Canyon*, V.T. Hamlin's *Alley Oop*, and Will Eisner's *The Spirit*. All of our published material is listed in a 32-page retail catalog available free by sending a card to:

Kitchen Sink Press
No. 2 Swamp Rd.
Princeton WI 54968

**A** HEAVY CRASHING NOISE REACHES THEIR EARS...SUDDENLY, A GIANT MAGNOPED LUMBERS INTO VIEW!..........

# FLASH GORDON

by ALEX RAYMOND

August 11, 1935
to
August 1, 1937

Strips 82-187

DRIVEN FROM AZURA'S PALACE, FLASH, DALE AND ZARKOV FLEE TO A SMALL HOVEL--A HERDSMAN ORDERS THEM AWAY

DESPERATELY IN NEED OF SHELTER FROM THE SHARP EYES OF AZURA'S SCOUT PATROLS, FLASH CLOSES IN ON THE PEASANT AND DROPS HIM WITH A SINGLE BLOW!

WE JUST GOT HERE IN TIME--THERE GOES A PATROL OF MAGIC MEN SEARCHING FOR US!

OH, FLASH, YOU COULD HAVE RULED SYK IF IT HADN'T BEEN FOR ME!

I'D RATHER HAVE YOU THAN SIX KINGDOMS!

WHAT'LL WE EVER DO? ESCAPE FROM THIS WILD LAND IS IMPOSSIBLE--AND WE COULDN'T HOPE TO CONQUER AZURA UNAIDED

IF I COULD ONLY FINISH MY MACHINE FOR BENDING AND DESTROYING LIGHT------

WHAT DO YOU NEED? I'LL RAID ONE OF AZURA'S SIGNAL STATIONS

FLASH, WITH A LIST OF THE REQUIRED MACHINERY, MOUNTS THE PEASANT'S HORSE AND SETS OUT ON HIS PERILOUS MISSION

AT DAWN----

OH, THANK HEAVEN, HE'S SAFE--I WAS SO WORRIED!---

HE MUST HAVE TAKEN ANOTHER HORSE AND A CART FROM THE GARRISON--THAT LAD IS SUPERB!

ALEX RAYMOND
8-11
© 1935, King Features Syndicate, Inc., Great Britain rights reserved

AFTER TWO DAYS AND NIGHTS OF FEVERISH WORK, FLASH AND ZARKOV COMPLETE THE LIGHT-MACHINE--FLASH TAKES HIS PLACE ON A PLATFORM--------

NEXT WEEK "THE AVENGING SHADOW"!

ZARKOV THROWS THE SWITCH--A HUGE BLUE SPARK LEAPS FROM THE ELECTRODES--FLASH SLOWLY DISAPPEARS FROM VIEW--ONLY HIS SHADOW REMAINS!

FLASH GORDON, MADE INVISIBLE BY ZARKOV'S RAY, MAKES A ONE-MAN WAR ON THE WITCH QUEEN, AZURA——————

A RUNAWAY HORSE!

I'LL STOP HIM!

OUTSIDE AZURA'S PALACE WALLS, THREE GUARDS SEE A RIDERLESS HORSE BEARING DOWN ON THEM——— FLASH, THOUGH INVISIBLE, CASTS A SHADOW——————

TAO'S CURSE IS UPON US!

FLASH'S HORSE STUMBLES AND FALLS——FLASH LUNGES AT THE OFFICER——THE OTHER SOLDIERS, SEEING ONLY FLASH'S SHADOW CAST ON THE WALL, FLEE IN STARK TERROR !—————

IT'S A SHADOW! A LIVING SHADOW OF DEATH!

FLASH DASHES AFTER ONE OF THE GUARDS AND FOLLOWS HIM THROUGH THE GATES————————

WELL, I GOT HIS GUN———— NOW FOR THE PALACE!

A S-S-SHADOW KILLED MY COMRADES——I CAME FOR HELP!

A SHADOW? YOU'RE DRUNK! GET BACK ON DUTY OR I'LL STRIP THE SKIN FROM YOUR BACK!

IN THE PALACE HALLS———— TWO OFFICERS STOP ONE OF THE FLEEING GUARDS——————

WHIRLING, THE OFFICERS SEE FLASH'S SHADOW——THEY REACH FOR THEIR GUNS———— FLASH DROPS THEM BEFORE THEY CAN DRAW————————

DROP THAT GUN, FOOL! YOU CANNOT KILL ME——— TELL AZURA THAT THE AVENGING SHADOW IS COMING!

FLASH MAKES HIS WAY TO THE BARRACKS——

8-18

©1935, King Features Syndicate, Inc., Great Britain rights reserved.

=NEXT WEEK=
"UNSEEN HORROR!"

FLASH GORDON, AS HIS INVISIBILITY WEARS OFF, DARINGLY KIDNAPS HIS ENEMY, THE WITCH QUEEN, AZURA--------

HOTLY PURSUED, FLASH LEAPS FROM THE WALL AND DASHES TOWARD THE HILLS------

THIS LOOKS LIKE A WAY OUT

NO, NO, FLASH! IT'S "THE PIT OF PERIL!"

SEEING A MYSTERIOUS DOOR SET IN THE SIDE OF A HILL, FLASH MAKES FOR IT------

OUR QUEEN--LOST IN THE PIT OF THE DEATH DWARFS!

BAR THE GATE OR THEY'LL GET US!

WELL, THEY'LL KILL THE SHADOW, TOO!

AZURA'S GUARDS HALT, TERRIFIED AND BAFFLED------

WHY ARE YOU SO FRIGHTENED, AZURA?

WE DROVE THE WARRIOR DWARFS DOWN INTO THESE PITS AND TUNNELS--WE EXECUTE PRISONERS BY THROWING THEM TO THE DWARFS!

FLASH DUCKS BEHIND A ROCK--A HAIRY HORDE OF GORILLA-ARMED HORRORS BURSTS INTO VIEW AND, WITH VENGEFUL CRIES, SLOWLY ADVANCES TOWARD THEIR HATED WITCH QUEEN!

÷ NEXT WEEK :- "THE DEATH DWARFS!"

FLASH--YOUR HEAD! I CAN SEE IT!

I'M SORRY TO HEAR THAT--MY REMAINING INVISIBLE IS OUR BIG HOPE----

OH, FLASH, TAKE ME BACK--I'LL MAKE YOU KING! I'LL OBEY YOU FOREVER----

TOO LATE, AZURA--HERE THEY COME! LET THEM CAPTURE YOU--I'LL BE NEAR

9-8

12

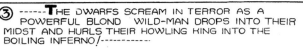

③ ------THE DWARFS SCREAM IN TERROR AS A POWERFUL BLOND WILD-MAN DROPS INTO THEIR MIDST AND HURLS THEIR HOWLING KING INTO THE BOILING INFERNO!------------

------FLASH GORDON, NOW FULLY VISIBLE, DECIDES ON A DESPERATE ATTEMPT TO SAVE HER---------

④ WHAT CAN WE DO NOW? WE'RE TRAPPED---

JUMP ON MY BACK AND HOLD TIGHT!

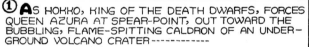

① AS HOKKO, KING OF THE DEATH DWARFS, FORCES QUEEN AZURA AT SPEAR-POINT, OUT TOWARD THE BUBBLING, FLAME-SPITTING CALDRON OF AN UNDER-GROUND VOLCANO CRATER------------

⑤ USING HOKKO'S SPEAR AS A VAULTING-POLE, FLASH SOARS OVER THE ENRAGED DWARFS------

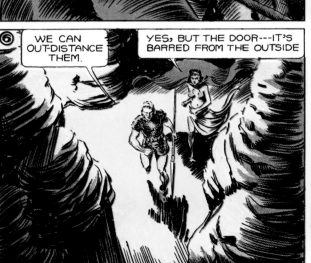

⑥ WE CAN OUT-DISTANCE THEM.

YES, BUT THE DOOR---IT'S BARRED FROM THE OUTSIDE

⑦ HELP! OH, HELP! IT'S ME, QUEEN AZURA!

NO USE, AZURA--HERE THEY COME! STAND BEHIND ME--I'LL HOLD THEM OFF AS LONG AS I CAN------

9-22

----: NEXT WEEK :----
"THE GREEN-EYED DRAGON!"

14

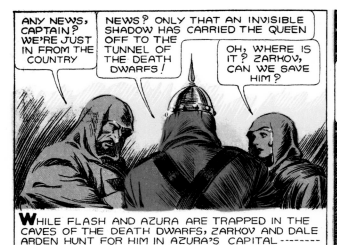

WHILE FLASH AND AZURA ARE TRAPPED IN THE CAVES OF THE DEATH DWARFS, ZARKOV AND DALE ARDEN HUNT FOR HIM IN AZURA'S CAPITAL --------

OUTSIDE THE BARRED ENTRANCE TO THE DWARF'S TUNNEL ------

WHILE INSIDE THE DOOR -----

DR. ZARKOV PUSHES FLASH AND AZURA OUTSIDE AND SENDS BOLT AFTER BOLT CRASHING INTO THE RANKS OF THE SCREAMING DWARFS

-: NEXT WEEK :-
"THE AMBUSH!"

9-29

DALE, YOU KNOW I LOVE YOU--THE ONLY REASON I KISSED HER WAS BECAUSE SHE ASKED ME TO---WE THOUGHT WE WERE DYING!

SUCH CHIVALRY! YOU DON'T KNOW WHAT LOVE MEANS, FLASH GORDON---IT IS AZURA YOU LOVE--LET ME GO--I HATE YOU!

FLASH AND AZURA, TRAPPED BY THE DEATH DWARFS, KISS EACH OTHER FAREWELL--ZARKOV AND DALE APPEAR AT THAT MOMENT AND RESCUE THEM--------

AN OFFICER, COMMANDING A SCOUTING PATROL, SPOTS THE THREE FUGITIVES AND THEIR CAPTIVE--------

AT A SIGNAL FROM THE CAPTAIN, THE SOLDIERS DISMOUNT AND FILE TOWARD A NARROW RAVINE----------

THEY TAKE THEIR POSITIONS ON OPPOSITE SIDES OF THE RAVINE-------

AS THE FUGITIVES ENTER THE PASSAGE, THEY CHARGE WITH LEVELED FLAME GUNS!----

HALT! ON YOUR KNEES TO YOUR QUEEN!

THEN, TO THE UTTER SURPRISE OF FLASH, DALE AND ZARKOV, THE CAPTIVE QUEEN PLACES HERSELF BEFORE THEM!-----------

THE EARTHMAN HAS SAVED MY LIFE, CAPTAIN---HE IS HENCEFORTH YOUR KING, IN FACT AS WELL AS IN NAME--- FLASH GORDON AND HIS FRIENDS ARE TO BE ESCORTED TO MY PALACE IN HONOR AND SAFETY!

IT IS MY DUTY TO WARN YOU, MY QUEEN, THAT IN YOUR ABSENCE, TAHL HAS SEIZED THE THRONE--- THE ARMY REMAINS LOYAL TO YOU

FLASH GORDON, KING OF KIRA, THE CAVE WORLD, RIDES INTO SYK AT THE HEAD OF AZURA'S TROOPS THEY ARE GREETED BY A TREACHEROUS SILENCE!

-NEXT WEEK- "A LOST KINGDOM!"

16

① HAVING WON HIS KINGDOM, FLASH AWAITS AN ANSWER TO HIS ATTEMPT TO GAIN THE OFFICIAL RECOGNITION OF MING THE MERCILESS, EMPEROR OF MONGO——————

WHAT IS IT, CAPTAIN?

A VISARADIOGRAM FROM MING, THE MERCILESS, SIRE

②

"TO FLASH GORDON, GREETINGS: YOUR BID TO BE RECOGNIZED AS KING OF KIRA, THE CAVE WORLD, REJECTED UNTIL YOU DISPOSE OF THE PRESENT RULER, WHO, YOU CLAIM, HAS ABDICATED IN YOUR FAVOR——SUCH AN EVENT IS HIGHLY IMPROBABLE——YOUR LYING IMPUDENCE AMAZES ME!"

SIGNED, MING THE MERCILESS, SUPREME EMPEROR OF MONGO

③ YOU WILL SEND THE FOLLOWING MESSAGE TO MING: "TO PROVE MY RANK AS KING OF KIRA, AND IN ANSWER TO YOUR INSULTING MESSAGE TO ME, I HEREBY DECLARE THAT A STATE OF WAR EXISTS BETWEEN YOUR COUNTRY AND MINE!"

④

FLASH'S ARMY, THOUSANDS STRONG, MOVES TOWARD THE SURFACE WORLD OF MONGO——KHAN, THE HAWK-MAN, HEADS THE INFANTRY

⑤ DR. ZARKOV, THE SCIENTIFIC GENIUS FROM THE EARTH, HEADS QUEEN AZURA'S MAGNIFICENT ARTILLERY UNITS————————

© 1935, King Features Syndicate, Inc. Great Britain rights reserved

⑥

FLASH AND DALE HEAD THE FAMED BLACK LANCERS IN A GREAT OFFENSIVE AGAINST THE TYRANT OF MONGO!

—NEXT WEEK—
MING'S WRATH!

18

① FLASH AND DALE ADVANCE TO MEET THE ARMIES OF MING, THE MERCILESS-- HEARING THE THROB OF APPROACHING ROCKET SHIPS--------------

-----FLASH SIGNALS TO HIS MEN TO TAKE AN OPEN FORMATION TO MAKE AS SMALL A TARGET AS POSSIBLE-------------

② HUGE, GLISTENING, ROCKET DREADNOUGHTS, THE PRIDE OF MING'S AIR FLEET, ROAR INTO VIEW--THE LEADER SPIES FLASH'S ARMY-------------

④ MEANWHILE, IN A SIGNAL TOWER HIGH IN THE STRATOSPHERE, EMPEROR MING WATCHES THE DEADLY GAME-----------

THE FOOLS! CAN'T THEY SEE THAT HIDDEN ARTILLERY? SEND OUT A WARNING!

11·3

© 1933, King Features Syndicate, Inc., Great Britain rights reserved ®

③ FROM HIS POSITION ATOP ONE OF HIS CONCEALED ARTILLERY UNITS, DR. ZARKOV WAVES A SIGNAL TO HIS BATTERY COMMANDERS-----------

⑤ BUT THE WARNING COMES TOO LATE--THE MAMMOTH GUN SNOUTS BELCH A FIERY GREETING TO THE DIVING SHIPS--THE VERY PLANET ROCKS UNDER THE FURIOUS BARRAGE-----------

⑥ SECRET RAYS, KNOWN ONLY TO DR. ZARKOV, CUT OFF THE ROCKET MOTORS--GREAT BOLTS OF ELECTRICITY, AIDED BY BOLTS OF CONCENTRATED SOUND, TEAR THE ONCE PROUD FLEET TO SHREDS!
-NEXT WEEK- **MING'S BRAND OF DEATH!**

VULTAN! MY FRIEND! I'M SURE GLAD TO SEE YOU, YOU OLD RASCAL!

I HEARD THAT YOU AND MING WERE AT IT AGAIN, SO I BROUGHT THE BOYS ALONG TO HELP OUT!

JUST AS MING AND ORAX LAUNCH THEIR FLAMING DEATH, FLASH RECEIVES REINFORCEMENTS------

KING FLASH! THE FIRE PEOPLE HAVE DESTROYED YOUR RIGHT FLANK!

GO TO THE REAR AND ORDER ZARKOV TO GET THE ARTILLERY GOING---THE HAWKMEN WILL ATTACK AFTER THE FIRST BARRAGE!

THE ASBESTOS-CLAD FIRE PEOPLE MARCH RUTHLESSLY THROUGH THEIR NATIVE ELEMENT, A ROARING SEA OF FLAME----THE STRAGGLING REMNANTS OF FLASH'S RIGHT FLANK FALL BACK AGAINST THE TREMENDOUS ODDS------

A SQUADRON OF GALLANT BLACK LANCERS CHARGES INTO CERTAIN DEATH IN A DESPERATE ATTEMPT TO STEM THE TIDE--------

BUT THE WHIRLING, DIVING HAWKMEN HALT THE FIRE PEOPLE FOR A MOMENT-------

NEXT WEEK: THE CONQUEST OF FIRE!

12-1

24

THE HAWKMEN ARE SPEARING THE FIRE PEOPLE FROM THE AIR---THERE IS ONLY ONE WAY TO DEAL WITH THEM

MING, THE MERCILESS, AND ORAX, THE FIRE KING, WATCH THE PROGRESS OF THE BATTLE THROUGH A TELEVISOR

POLARIZED BEAMS OF LIGHT, ACTING AS GIGANTIC MAGNETS ON THE ARMOR OF THE HAWKMEN, DRAW THEM DOWN INTO THE RAGING FLAMES!

VERY WELL, ORDER A RETREAT--TAKE DALE BACK TO ZARKOV AND TELL HIM TO PROTECT HER WITH HIS LIFE---I HAVE AN IDEA --- OUR LAST HOPE!

THE GUNS ARE TOO HOT TO HANDLE, SIRE-- ZARKOV SUGGESTS A RETREAT

OH, DARLING, PLEASE DON'T DO ANYTHING FOOLISH--

A WOUNDED ARTILLERY OFFICER BRINGS A LAST DESPAIRING MESSAGE TO HIS KING, FLASH GORDON

STRAPPING A HEAVY ATOM GUN ON HIS BACK, FLASH STRUGGLES DES-PERATELY UP THE MOUNTAIN-SIDE---

HE TRAINS THE GUN ON A HUGE DAM HOLDING BACK MILLIONS OF TONS OF WATER ---

12-8

© 1935, King Features Syndicate, Inc., Great Britain rights reserved.

AN INFERNO OF WATER AND STEAM FLOODS THE VALLEY BELOW, SWEEPING OVER THE ARMY OF FIRE PEOPLE LIKE A HUGE TIDAL WAVE ---

NEXT WEEK: BETRAYED!

ALEX RAYMOND

24

NEXT WEEK:
**A KING IN PRISON!**

26

1 FLASH GORDON, CAPTURED BY EMPEROR MING, THE MERCILESS, IS PLACED IN AN UNDERGROUND DUNGEON, THERE TO MEET A HORRIBLE CONSTRICTOSAURUS------

DO WE HAVE TO WAIT 'TIL MIDNIGHT? FLASH MAY BE DYING----------

OUR ONLY CHANCE IS TO FLY TO MING'S PALACE IN THE DARKNESS-----

2 MEANTIME, DR. ZARKOV SEIZES ONE OF MING'S SMALL ABANDONED ROCKET SHIPS---AFTER REPAIRING IT, HE AND DALE PAINT THE SHIP A DEAD BLACK TO MAKE IT INVISIBLE FOR NIGHT FLYING-----------

3 AT NIGHTFALL, THE RESCUE SHIP TAKES OFF---------

4 OH, DR. ZARKOV, IF WE'RE ONLY IN TIME!

WE'RE NEARING MING'S CAPITAL---I'M SWITCHING FROM ROCKETS TO COMPRESSED AIR, SO THE FLAME FROM OUR ROCKET TUBES WON'T GIVE US AWAY--------

THERE'S MING'S PALACE---I'D LIKE TO DROP SOME ATOM BOMBS ON THAT PLACE!

BUT WE MIGHT HIT FLASH---WHERE DO WE LAND?

© 1935, King Features Syndicate, Inc., Great Britain rights reserved

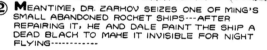
DOWN IN THE DUNGEONS, FLASH FIGHTS FOR HIS LIFE AGAINST THE WRITHING BEAST----------

HE WAS A TOUGH ONE TO KILL---BUT, THANK GOODNESS, THEY PUT A LONG CHAIN ON MY WRISTS---HELLO, A LOOSE BOLT! I MUST HAVE PULLED IT LOOSE DURING THE FIGHT!

NEXT WEEK THE MISSING KING

AFTER UNSUCCESSFULLY INVADING MING'S EMPIRE, FLASH IS CAPTURED AND IMPRISONED WITH A HORRIBLE CONSTRICTOSAURUS---HE STRANGLES THE BEAST WITH HIS CHAINS AND, IN DOING SO, LOOSENS ONE OF THE BOLTS THAT HOLDS HIM TO THE WALL---DESPERATELY, HE FIGHTS HIS BONDS-----------

SUCCESS SO FAR----NOW FOR THE DOOR!

I CAN'T FORCE THIS DOOR---THIS CALLS FOR STRATEGY-----

FLASH ATTEMPTS TO FORCE THE LOCK WITH A BOLT FROM HIS CHAINS-----------

QUICK --- GUARD, I'M DYING--- GET ME A DRINK--- I'LL TELL YOU WHERE MY GOLD IS HIDDEN WATER----- WATER! YOU DON'T NEED TO WORRY ABOUT---- THE---- ANIMAL---I ---I----- CHOKED IT-----

GOLD? YOU TELL ME FIRST, AND I'LL GET YOU A DRINK!

COMPLETELY FOOLED, THE GUARD OPENS THE DOOR----- FLASH SWINGS HIS HEAVY CHAINS--------

-----LATER, MING COMES TO TAUNT HIS PRISONER-----

IT'S THE GUARD! FLASH GORDON HAS ESCAPED! CALL OUT THE TROOPS!

NEXT WEEK: THE DEATH TRAIL!

1-5

FLASH ESCAPES FROM MING'S DUNGEON AND FLEES TO THE CITY---- MING ORDERS HIS OFFICERS TO RE-CAPTURE HIM OR FACE THE TORTURERS

CLOSE THE ELECTRIC GATES--- ELECTRIFY THE CITY WALLS! NO ONE SHALL LEAVE 'TIL WE HAVE COMBED THE CITY FOR FLASH GORDON !

MING SURROUNDS HIS CITY WITH A RING OF FIRE------

WE'RE STRANGERS HERE---IS IT TRUE THAT HIS SUPREME INTELLIGENCE HAS CAPTURED THE EARTHMAN, FLASH GORDON ?

YES, BUT THE REBEL HAS ESCAPED---WATCH FOR HIM AND YOU'LL BE RE-WARDED

WE CERTAINLY WILL

MEANTIME, DALE AND DR. ZARKOV, BENT ON RESCUING FLASH, HAVE LANDED SECRETLY IN THE CITY

OPEN THE GATES---I HAVE BUSINESS OUT-SIDE------

FOOL! NO MAN CAN ENTER OR PASS THE FLAME GATES--- MING, HIMSELF, HAS LOCKED THE CITY------SAY------YOU'RE FLASH GORDON !

AN OFFICER OF THE GUARD RECOGNIZES THE FLEEING KING------

FLASH DROPS HIS CAPE ON THE OFFICER'S LUNGING SWORD, THEN, PICKING HIM UP BODILY, HURLS HIM, SCREAMING, THROUGH THE ELECTRIC GATE !

IN A FEW MOMENTS, THE CITY STREETS CRAWL WITH A SEETHING MASS OF HOWL-ING SOLDIERS, ALL DEMAND-ING FLASH'S BLOOD---FLASH CROUCHES IN HIS HIDING-PLACE AND SWEARS NEVER TO BE CAP-TURED ALIVE !

NEXT WEEK.
IN DISGUISE !

1-12

WHEN FLASH, DISGUISED AS A SOLDIER, IS PICKED UP BY A DETAIL OF MING'S GUARDSMEN, DALE AND ZARKOV FOLLOW———

THOSE TWO HAVE FOLLOWED US FAR ENOUGH—— ARREST THEM!

THERE GOES FLASH GORDON AROUND THAT CORNER! COME ON, MEN, LET'S GET THAT REWARD!

FLASH, OUTNUMBERED, TRIES A DESPERATE TRICK——

WHY WERE YOU FOLLOWING US? WHO ARE YOU? SHOW ME YOUR PASSPORTS!

WHY———WE JUST CAME TO TOWN TO SEE A———

FLASH DODGES INTO A SHOP, IN THE BAZAAR, AROUND THE CORNER———

———IN A SECOND, THE BAZAAR IS FILLED WITH SHOUTING SOLDIERS———

THE BRUTAL OFFICER TWISTS DALE TO HER KNEES——— ZARKOV REACHES FOR HIS SWORD——— FLASH STARTS FORWARD, BUT IS CHECKED BY ONE OF HIS COMPANIONS———

COME ON, SWEETHEART——— YOUR PASSPORT—OR JAIL!

EASY, FELLOW——— BETTER LET THE CAPTAIN HANDLE THIS!

DID YOU SEE FLASH GORDON JUST NOW, STOREKEEPER?

THE REBEL KING? NO———

NEXT WEEK: INTO THE JAWS OF DEATH!

WHAT CAN I SELL YOU?

I'M LOOKING FOR A COSTUME FOR THE GUARDSMEN'S BALL---- HAVE YOU ANY BEGGARS' OUTFITS?

AFTER A NARROW ESCAPE, FLASH DECIDES TO CHANGE HIS DISGUISE------

A NOVEL COSTUME, SOLDIER ----THAT WILL COST YOU TEN MINGOS ----

TEN MINGOS? VERY REASONABLE-- CHARGE IT TO THE EMPEROR!

THANK YOU---TELL ME--WASN'T SOMEBODY ARRESTED HERE JUST NOW?

YES--A MAN AND A WOMAN WERE TAKEN TO THE PALACE

FLASH MAKES HIS WAY TO THE CORNER WHERE DALE AND DR. ZARKOV WERE ARRESTED---------

YOUR SUPREME INTELLIGENCE, THESE TWO WERE ACTING SUSPICIOUSLY----

ZARKOV! AND MY SWEET LITTLE DALE! CAPTAIN, YOU HAVE DONE WELL!

MEANTIME, AT THE PALACE

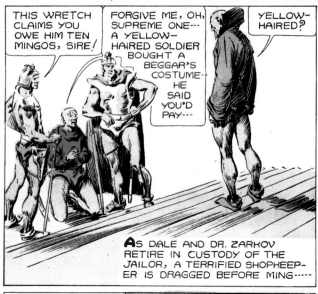

THIS WRETCH CLAIMS YOU OWE HIM TEN MINGOS, SIRE!

FORGIVE ME, OH, SUPREME ONE--- A YELLOW-HAIRED SOLDIER BOUGHT A BEGGAR'S COSTUME-- HE SAID YOU'D PAY---

YELLOW-HAIRED?

AS DALE AND DR. ZARKOV RETIRE IN CUSTODY OF THE JAILOR, A TERRIFIED SHOPKEEPER IS DRAGGED BEFORE MING-----

YOU FOOL! THAT WAS FLASH GORDON! TO THE DUNGEONS WITH HIM! ARREST OR KILL EVERY BEGGAR IN THE CITY!

-----AND FLASH, TRAILING DALE AND DR. ZARKOV, WALKS INTO THE PALACE TRAP!

NEXT WEEK: **A DARING GAMBLE!**

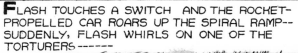

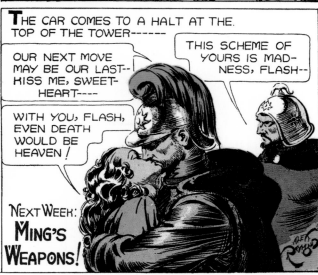

**1** INSTEAD OF TRYING TO ESCAPE FROM THE CITY, FLASH, DISGUISED AS MING'S COLONEL, TAKES DALE AND ZARKOV TO THE TOWER CONTROL-ROOM---

NO ADMITTANCE!

BY MING'S ORDERS-- CALL YOUR CHIEF, FELLOW!

**2** PLEASE PARDON THE GUARD'S RUDENESS, COLONEL--WE MUST BE CAREFUL HERE--

QUITE ALL RIGHT, CAPTAIN--MING WANTS THESE TWO GUESTS SHOWN HIS LATEST WEAPONS--

**3** --THIS DESTRUCTOPLANE IS OUR LATEST ACHIEVEMENT, SIR--WE CAN INSTANTLY LOCATE, AND BLAST INTO FRAGMENTS, ANY AIRCRAFT AT ANY DISTANCE--

THE OFFICER LEADS FLASH AND HIS FRIENDS THROUGH A VAST ROOM FILLED WITH SPOTLESS MACHINERY AND MIGHTY ENGINES OF DESTRUCTION------

**4** SHOW OUR GUESTS HOW WE PROTECT THIS ROOM FROM ATTACK, CAPTAIN--

INSIDE A PILLAR OVER THERE, A MAN IS ALWAYS STATIONED, TO USE THE PARALYZO RAY----

**5** IF AN ENEMY BREAKS IN, WE PARALYZE EVERY-ONE--IT IS HARMLESS, BUT LASTS HALF AN HOUR--BEHOLD!

THE CAPTAIN THROWS THE SWITCH-- FLASH, DALE AND ZAR-KOV WATCH THE DETECTOPLATE

**6** THE ATMOSPHERE IN THE OUTER ROOM TURNS GREENISH AND THE GUARDS STIFFEN AT THEIR STATIONS------

© 1936, King Features Syndicate, Inc., Great Britain rights reserved

**7** NICE WORK, CAPTAIN--THE JOKE'S ON YOU! DON'T MOVE, OR YOU DIE!

NEXT WEEK: **A POST OF PERIL!**

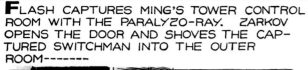

FLASH CAPTURES MING'S TOWER CONTROL ROOM WITH THE PARALYZO-RAY. ZARKOV OPENS THE DOOR AND SHOVES THE CAPTURED SWITCHMAN INTO THE OUTER ROOM-------

QUICK, ZARKOV-- SHUT THE DOOR!

STEPPING INTO THE ROOM, THE UNLUCKY CAPTIVE IS HIT BY THE RAY------

FLASH AND ZARKOV BIND THE CAPTURED COMMANDER OF THE TOWER CONTROL ROOM-------

TURN OFF THE RAY, ZARKOV--GO OUT AND TIE UP THE GUARDS.

WE MUST HURRY-- THEY'LL RECOVER IN HALF AN HOUR.

I'LL BE LOOKOUT.

HAVING BOUND THE PARALYZED PERSONNEL OF THE CONTROL ROOM, ZARKOV DRAGS THEM BEHIND A HUGE PILLAR------

THESE LADS WON'T MOVE EVEN AFTER THEY COME TO---WHAT NEXT?

CHECK UP ON MING'S WEAPONS--I'M CALLING OUR ARMY ON THE SPACEOPHONE------ HELLO, BARIN------

FLASH! BY TAO, WHERE ARE YOU?

IN FLASH'S DISTANT ARMY CAMP------

LOOK, VULTAN--- FLASH IS STILL ALIVE!

GREAT! WHAT DOES HE WANT US TO DO?

TAKE THE ARMY TO BARIN'S TREE KING- DOM--- I'LL MEET YOU THERE.

3-1

--AND JUST HOW WILL YOU GET PAST MING'S GUARDS?

I'LL INVITE MING UP HERE. MAYBE HE'LL HELP US!

OH, FLASH--WHAT MAD RISK ARE YOU GOING TO TAKE NOW?

NEXT WEEK:
**THE BAITED TRAP!**

"I'VE JUST CAPTURED FLASH GORDON, YOUR SUPREME INTELLIGENCE--IF YOU WANT TO SEE HIM BEFORE HE DIES, YOU'D BETTER COME UP HERE"

FLASH FORCES THE ONE CONSCIOUS GUARD TO SUMMON MING TO THE CONTROL TOWER------

"REMEMBER--KILL EVERYONE AT THE FIRST SIGN OF TROUBLE!"

BUT MING PROVES HIS RIGHT TO THE TITLE OF "SUPREME INTELLIGENCE" AS HE PREPARES AGAINST TREACHERY-----

"AH, CAPTAIN LUONG, I'VE BEEN WAITING FOR THIS MOMENT--I MUST NOT MISS IT!"

"YES, HE'S DYING----"

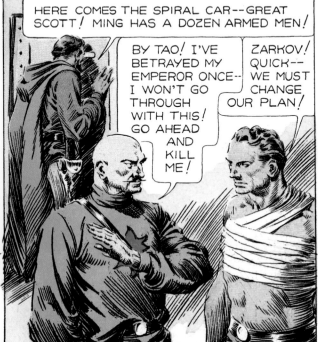

"HERE COMES THE SPIRAL CAR--GREAT SCOTT! MING HAS A DOZEN ARMED MEN!"

"BY TAO! I'VE BETRAYED MY EMPEROR ONCE--I WON'T GO THROUGH WITH THIS! GO AHEAD AND KILL ME!"

"ZARKOV! QUICK-- WE MUST CHANGE OUR PLAN!"

"OH, FLASH, PLEASE DON'T TRY TO GO THROUGH WITH THIS-- IT'S MADNESS!"

"IT'S OUR ONLY CHANCE, DALE--THIS WAY, WE AT LEAST HAVE A FIGHTING CHANCE--YOU'D BETTER TAKE YOUR PLACE INSIDE THE PILLAR--"

HASTILY BINDING AND GAGGING CAPTAIN LUONG, ZARKOV DONS HIS UNIFORM AND TAKES HIS PLACE AS MING POUNDS IMPATIENTLY ON THE DOOR------

"ENTER, YOUR SUPREME INTELLIGENCE----"

3-8

NEXT WEEK: LIFE OR DEATH?

FLASH FINALLY RECOVERS FROM THE PARALYZO-RAY------

DALE, DARLING, IF IT WASN'T FOR YOUR QUICK WIT, MING WOULD HAVE KILLED ALL OF US!

I HATED TO PARALYZE YOU AND ZARKOV, BUT IT WAS THE ONLY WAY

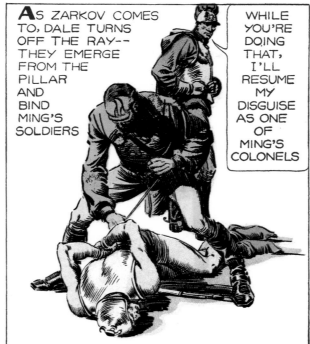

AS ZARKOV COMES TO, DALE TURNS OFF THE RAY-- THEY EMERGE FROM THE PILLAR AND BIND MING'S SOLDIERS

WHILE YOU'RE DOING THAT, I'LL RESUME MY DISGUISE AS ONE OF MING'S COLONELS

SO, FLASH GORDON--- YOU HAVE TRICKED ME!

NO, MING--DALE TRAPPED YOU--A GIRL TAKES MONGO'S EMPEROR PRISONER!

NOW, MY FRIEND, YOU'LL ESCORT US OUT OF YOUR CITY OR YOU'LL DIE RIGHT HERE!

I REFUSE! YOU FOOL EARTH-MEN WOULD NEVER KILL A PRISONER--YOU'RE TOO CHICKEN-HEARTED!

NO USE, ZARKOV--

THIS IS THE ONLY WAY!

3-22

PRETENDING TO BE GUARDED BY THE UNCONSCIOUS MING, THEY ENTER THE SPIRAL CAR--FLASH STARTS THE ROCKETS AND THEY ROAR DOWN THE INCLINE-----

NEXT WEEK: DISASTER!

CAN WE RUN THIS CAR THROUGH THE STREETS?

I'LL TRY

FLASH HAS PARALYZED THE CAP-TURED MING AND HOPES TO BLUFF HIS WAY OUT OF THE CITY-------

AS THE CAR SPEEDS THROUGH THE STREETS THE UNSUSPECTING TOWNSPEOPLE SALUTE THEIR EMPEROR-----

AS THEY APPROACH A GROUP OF ARMED GUARDSMEN, MING SUDDENLY LEAPS TO HIS FEET--------

GUARDS! STOP THIS CAR! SHOOT THESE THREE PRISONERS!

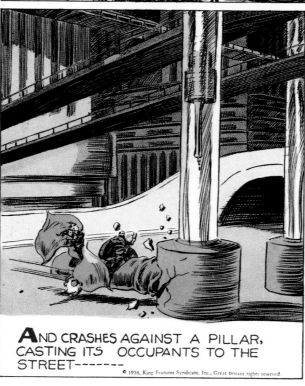

FLASH GIVES THE CAR THE GUN--IT CAREENS WILDLY THROUGH THE PANIC-STRICKEN GUARDS-------

AND CRASHES AGAINST A PILLAR, CASTING ITS OCCUPANTS TO THE STREET-------

WHILE FLASH HOLDS OFF THE ENRAGED SOLDIERS, DALE AND ZARKOV SLIP INTO A PRIVATE HOME---

NEXT WEEK: ESCAPE!

3-29

LEAD ME TO THE BACK DOOR, QUICK! AND NO TREACHERY, OR ELSE--!

DON'T HURT HIM--

DON'T KILL ME-- I'LL DO ANY-THING YOU SAY!

**H**OTLY PURSUED BY MING'S GUARDS, FLASH LEADS DALE AND ZARKOV INTO A PRIVATE HOME--------

**A**S THE SHIP ROARS FROM ITS HANGAR, EVERY BATTERY IN THE CITY OPENS FIRE-----

**T**HE THREE FUGITIVES ESCAPE INTO AN ALLEY-------

HURRY! THERE'S THE PLACE I HID OUR ROCKET SHIP

**Z**ARKOV RETAL-IATES WITH A FEW WELL-PLACED DISSOLVO-RAYS AS A PARTING GESTURE------

**T**HEY ENTER A HANGAR, FORMERLY THE PROPERTY OF PRINCE BARIN, WHICH HOUSES ZARKOV'S BLACK ROCKET SHIP--ZARKOV PRESSES A BUTTON-- THE HUGE DOORS SLIDE OPEN-----

**M**ING'S AIR FLEET QUICKLY FOLLOWS AS ZARKOV HEADS INTO THE STRANGE MANY-HUED FOGS-------

4-5

NEXT WEEK:
# THE SEA OF MYSTERY!

"SO THIS IS THE FAMOUS "SEA OF MYSTERY" THAT THE AIRMEN FEAR SO MUCH!

MING'S AIR FLEET WILL NEVER FIND US HERE!

HAVING ESCAPED FROM MING'S CITY, FLASH, DALE AND DR. ZARKOV HEAD INTO THE TREACHEROUS FOGS WHICH COVER THE "SEA OF MYSTERY"

QUICK, FLASH, OPEN THAT DOOR — WE'LL HAVE TO JUMP AND TAKE OUR CHANCES! DROWNING IS BETTER THAN BEING ROASTED ALIVE!

SUDDENLY, THE SHIP LURCHES WILDLY AND CHANGES ITS COURSE

THEY'RE RIGHT TO SHUN THIS SEA — OUR INSTRUMENTS HAVE GONE CRAZY!

THE ROCKET SHIP PLUNGES, HISSING, INTO THE SEA, NEAR A ROCKY REEF

© 1936, King Features Syndicate, Inc., Great Britain rights reserved.
 4-12

FROM THE MYSTERIOUS DEPTHS OF THE SEA, A MAGNETO-RAY SEIZES THE ROCKET SHIP — ITS NOSE GLOWS HOTLY

FLASH! ZARKOV, WHERE'S FLASH?

HE — HE WENT DOWN LIKE A STONE, DALE — I COULDN'T REACH HIM

AFTER A BITTER STRUGGLE, DALE AND ZARKOV STAGGER ONTO A WAVE-LASHED ISLAND

NEXT WEEK:— 
INTO THE WATER WORLD!

FLASH CLINGS DESPERATELY TO A SECTION OF THE REEF UPON WHICH THE ROCKET SHIP CRASHED······THE HUNGRY SEA CLUTCHES AT HIS BODY·······

"HE IS AN AIR-BREATHER, QUEEN UNDINA······HE IS DROWNING·····"

"HE IS HANDSOME·····LET HIM LIVE, TRITON······BRING THE LUNG MACHINE!"

FLASH IS BROUGHT TO A CASTLE CARVED OUT OF SOLID CORAL AND ENCRUSTED WITH PEARLS AND PRECIOUS STONES·············

UNCONSCIOUSNESS FINALLY OVERTAKES HIM AND HE SINKS BENEATH THE SURFACE OF THE SEA OF MYSTERY·············

"HE IS A MAN OF UNUSUAL STRENGTH, MY QUEEN······HE RESPONDS TO OUR TREATMENT······"

"TAKE THE LUNG-MACHINE AWAY BEFORE HE WAKES·······BRING HIM TO MY CHAMBERS"

A HUGE MACHINE IS ROLLED INTO THE THRONE-ROOM·····FLASH IS PLACED INTO IT AND TRITON WORKS FEVERISHLY AT THE VALVES··········

IN THE DEPTHS OF THE WATER-WORLD A POWERFUL MAGNETO-RAY DRAWS HIS LIMP BODY TOWARD A BEAUTIFUL CORAL CITY·············

"YOU'RE NOT DROWNED···· BUT YOU'LL HAVE TO LIVE IN THE WATER WORLD FOREVER!"

"AM I DROWNED? ARE YOU A MERMAID?"

4-19

FLASH AWAKENS TO FIND HIMSELF BREATHING WATER IN AN UNDERSEA PALACE!··················

NEXT WEEK:
**LIFE UNDER THE SEA!**

44

DEEP IN THE WATERY WORLD OF THE SEA FOLK..........

YOU WERE TOO HANDSOME TO DROWN, SO WE CHANGED YOUR LUNGS TO BREATHE WATER.....

BUT.....NO, YOU CAN'T DO THAT! CHANGE ME BACK QUICK!

NOTHING CAN CHANGE YOU BACK.....YOU ARE ONE OF US FOREVER!

DOOMED TO A FISH'S LIFE! NEVER TO WALK IN THE OPEN AIR!.....AND SEPARATED FROM DALE FOREVER!

PLEASE DON'T BEAR A GRUDGE.....YOU'D HAVE DIED, IF IT WERE NOT FOR US.....COME, I WISH TO SEE YOUR SUNKEN SHIP.........

DID....DID YOU FIND DALE..... THE GIRL I MEAN?

THE SEA-QUEEN LEADS FLASH DOWN A CORRIDOR LEADING TO THE OPEN SEA............

THIS GIRL, DALE.....WHO IS SHE?

NEVER MIND THAT.....TELL ME WHETHER SHE'S ALIVE

AS UNDINA'S SOLDIERS ARE LOOTING THE SUNKEN ROCKET-SHIP, THERE IS A TERRIFIC RUSHING SOUND.....A CHARGING DEVOUROSAURUS!.....................

4-26

TRITON MEETS THEM AT THE WRECKED SHIP............

THE WOMAN AND THE OTHER MAN ESCAPED, QUEEN UNDINA

THANK HEAVENS! DALE AND ZARKOV ARE SAFE!

WE'LL ATTEND TO THEM LATER

SHOUTING TO THE OTHERS TO DASH FOR THE SHIP, FLASH DRAWS HIS SWORD AND WHIRLS TO FACE THE BEAST!.....................
NEXT WEEK:
# THE CANNIBAL MONSTER!

WITH ONE SWIPE OF ITS MIGHTY CLAW, THE DEVOUROSAURUS DISARMS FLASH AND FORCES HIM TO FLEE TO THE ROCKET SHIP⋯⋯⋯⋯⋯

NOW LET'S PRAY THAT THE COMBUSTION CHAMBERS ARE STILL DRY⋯⋯⋯⋯

SEIZED WITH AN IDEA, FLASH MAKES HIS WAY TO THE CONTROL-CABIN⋯⋯⋯HE JERKS THE THROTTLE DOWN⋯⋯⋯⋯ 5-3

HE CAN'T GET INTO THIS PASSAGEWAY⋯

WE HAVEN'T A CHANCE, EARTHMAN

HE'LL TEAR THE SHIP APART!

FLASH, QUEEN UNDINA AND TRITON HIDE IN A NARROW TUNNEL NEAR THE ROCKET TUBES⋯⋯⋯⋯

THERE IS A MUFFLED EXPLOSION⋯⋯THE MONSTER IS BLOWN TO BITS BUT THE WATER PRESSURE CAUSES THE ROCKETS TO BACKFIRE, TEARING THE SHIP APART!

MAD WITH THE BLOOD-THIRST, THE CANNIBAL MONSTER TEARS WILDLY AT THE ROCKET SHIP⋯⋯⋯⋯

LOOK, DALE!

DR. ZARKOV AND DALE, CASTAWAYS ON A NEARBY ISLE, ARE STARTLED BY THE GEYSER FROM THE EXPLOSION. **NEXT WEEK: THE EXPLORER**

FLUNG AGAINST THE ISLAND'S CORAL REEF IN THE EXPLOSION OF THE SUNKEN ROCKET SHIP, FLASH STARTS OUT IN SEARCH OF DALE AND ZARKOV

REACHING THE TOP OF THE REEF, FLASH SEES THE ISLAND

SMOKE! MAYBE DALE AND ZARKOV ARE SAFE

UNABLE TO BREATHE AIR, SINCE THE SEA FOLK ALTERED HIS LUNGS, FLASH CHOKES AND DROPS BACK INTO THE SEA

ONE MINUTE IN THE OPEN AIR AND I STRANGLE, I'M TRAPPED! I CAN'T EVEN TALK IN THE AIR!

REGAINING HIS BREATH, FLASH SWIMS AROUND TO THE OTHER SIDE OF THE ISLAND

UNABLE TO SHOUT, FLASH WAVES WILDLY TO HIS FRIENDS

THEY DON'T SEE ME

5-10

GOOD HEAVENS! I I CAN'T BELIEVE IT IT IS IT'S FLASH!

THANK GOODNESS FLASH! COME HERE!

FLASH THROWS A CHUNK OF CORAL DALE AND ZARKOV WHIRL AROUND

NEXT WEEK:
## PRISONERS OF TWO WORLDS

FLASH, HIS LUNGS CHANGED BY THE SEA FOLK, CANNOT TALK OR BREATHE, EXCEPT UNDER WATER

ZARKOV THINKS FLASH IS DROWNING AND TRIES TO RESCUE HIM FLASH MOTIONS HIM AWAY

FLASH FINALLY MAKES THE STRUGGLING SCIENTIST UNDERSTAND WHAT HAS HAPPENED

BEFORE FLASH CAN MOVE, HE IS SEIZED BY A HORRIBLE MONSTER OF THE DEEP—AN OCTOCLAW!

NEXT WEEK: **THE STRUGGLE!**

WEAPONLESS, FLASH BATTLES THE MAN-EATING OCTOCLAW····HE SLOWLY WEAKENS UNDER THE CRUSHING TENTACLES AND SLASHING CLAWS·········

AFTER TAKING DALE TO SAFETY ASHORE, ZARKOV GRABS A KNIFE AND RETURNS TO FLASH'S AID.

QUICK····GIVE ME THE KNIFE!

A MIGHTY TENTACLE FORCES THE AIR FROM ZARKOV'S LUNGS·····HE LOSES CONSCIOUSNESS········

FLASH GRABS ZARKOV'S KNIFE AND, WITH A LAST DESPERATE LUNGE, FATALLY WOUNDS THE MONSTER!·······

FLASH, MY LOVE····YOU'RE HURT····YOU'RE BLEEDING!

SWIMMING TO SHORE, FLASH DRAGS THE REVIVING ZARKOV TO THE BEACH···· DALE RUSHES TO MEET THEM·······

OH, ZARKOV, THIS IS HORRIBLE! HOW MUCH LONGER MUST WE BE SEPARATED?

HE HAS TO STAY UNDER WATER TO BREATHE NOW, DALE···· I HOPE HE CAN COME BACK TO US!

FLASH HAS TO HURRY BACK TO THE WATER TO WHICH THE SEA FOLK DOOMED HIM········

NEXT WEEK: **DIVIDED BY FATE!** 5-24

FLASH, CHANGED TO A WATER-BREATHER, DECIDES HE MUST RETURN TO THE SEA-FOLK..........

HE STEALS PAST THE DEAD OCTOCLAW, UPON WHICH FIERCE SHARKS ARE FEEDING...........

AFTER A TIME, FLASH COMES TO CORALIA, A CITY CARVED FROM SOLID CORAL....HE STOPS, STRUCK BY ITS BEAUTY........

LET ME IN.....I WISH TO SEE QUEEN UNDINA!

AT THE GATES OF THE UNDERSEA CITY, FLASH STRIKES A HUGE GONG, FASHIONED LIKE A SEA-SHELL...........

SO THE ROCKET BLAST DIDN'T KILL YOU EITHER? YOU'RE A TOUGH ONE!

WELCOME BACK TO CORALIA, EARTHMAN!

IN THE PALACE OF QUEEN UNDINA......

KNEEL, FLASH.... FOR SAVING ME AND TRITON, I MAKE THEE A NOBLE.......

HO, SLAVES! FOOD! MUSIC! REVELRY! BY ORDER OF THE QUEEN!

WE MUST CELEBRATE YOUR RETURN

THE CONDEMN-ED MAN ATE HEARTILY.......WHAT WOULDN'T I GIVE FOR ONE BREATH OF AIR!

NEXT WEEK:
**QUEENS CAN BE JEALOUS!**

5-31

TRANSFORMED INTO A WATER-BREATHER, FLASH IS MADE A NOBLE, AMID MUCH FEASTING AND REVELRY.

HOW DOES ONE DRINK FROM THIS?

TO OUR NEW NOBLE'S HEALTH!

SLIDE BACK THE COVER.........YOU HAVE MUCH TO LEARN, BUT YOU'LL LIKE IT HERE......I PROMISE YOU!

THAT LOOKS LIKE A LAND ANIMAL! HOW DO YOU CAPTURE THEM?

WE WEAR WATER-HELMETS WHEN WE HUNT ON THE ISLANDS........ BRING ME A HELMET!

PURIFIED WATER CIRCULATES THROUGH THE HEAD PIECE.

HM....M.........I'D LIKE TO GO EXPLORING ON AN ISLAND NEAR HERE

THAT REMINDS ME...THERE WAS A GIRL CALLED DALE IN YOUR SHIP......WE'LL ALL GO EXPLORING!

WHAT WILL YOU DO, IF YOU CAPTURE ANY ONE?

KILL THEM!

HELPLESS TO STOP UNDINA, FLASH RIDES WITH HER TO THE ISLAND REEF.........

NEXT WEEK :

THE MAN HUNT!

6-7

IF THEY WEREN'T DROWNED, WHY BOTHER THEM? THEY CANNOT HARM THE SEA QUEEN!

DO NOT PRESUME TO ADVISE ME, FLASH! YOU MAY HAVE BEEN A KING IN MONGO, BUT YOU ARE ONLY MY SUBJECT NOW!

FLASH TRIES TO SAVE DALE AND ZARKOV BY THREATENING UNDINA, QUEEN OF THE SEA-FOLK.............

TO SAVE HIS QUEEN, A SOLDIER WARILY RISES FROM HIS HIDING-PLACE AND FIRES HIS WATER-PRESSURE GUN AT FLASH!.............

THE JET SHATTERS FLASH'S WATER-HELMET.....ROBBED OF THE WATER, WHICH HE NOW BREATHES, HE CHOKES IN MERE AIR......

AT UNDINA'S ORDERS, FLASH IS RUSHED TO THE LIFE-GIVING WATER, AND TROOPS BIND DALE AND THE STRUGGLING ZARKOV!.............

NEXT WEEK.
TRIED FOR TREASON

6-21

THANKS FOR SAVING MY LIFE, TRITON...... BUT LIFE MEANS NOTHING TO ME, IF THEY HARM DALE.....

THAT'S UP TO QUEEN UNDINA

BACK IN THE WATER, WHICH IS ALL HE CAN BREATHE, FLASH RECOVERS CONSCIOUSNESS..........

THE QUEEN RETURNS TO CORALIA WITH HER PRISONERS.....DALE AND DR. ZARKOV ARE CARRIED IN AIR TANKS, SLUNG BETWEEN SEA-HORSES.........

LORD PLUTON, YOU MAY READ THE CHARGES AGAINST THESE PRISONERS

AS ROYAL SHERIFF OF CORALIA, I CHARGE THESE PRISONERS WITH TREASON AGAINST QUEEN UNDINA........

IN THE ROYAL JUDGMENT HALL..........

6-28

QUEEN UNDINA, I'M NOT GUILTY OF TREASON....I'M A KING OF MONGO..... BUT PUNISH ME AND FREE MY INNOCENT FRIENDS!

I SENTENCE THEM TO BE CHANGED TO WATER-BREATHERS TO THE PRISONS WITH THE THREE OF YOU!

1936, King Features Syndicate, Inc., World rights reserved

FORGIVE ME FOR GETTING YOU INTO THIS, DALE..... AND ZARKOV

I'M GLAD, FLASH.... I'LL BE IN THE SAME WORLD AS YOU!

SUFFER A SEA-CHANGE, INTO SOMETHING RICH AND STRANGE......

AND SO FLASH AND HIS FRIENDS ARE LEFT TO THE TENDER MERCIES OF PLUTON

NEXT WEEK: **PLUTON'S PRISON**

54

NEXT WEEK

IN THE ENEMY'S HALLS

7-12

LOOK OUT! SAVE DALE, FLASH.... NEVER MIND ME!

BEFORE FLASH, DALE AND ZARKOV CAN MAKE THEIR ESCAPE FROM THE PRISON, ONE OF THE STUNNED GUARDS SUDDENLY COMES TO LIFE........

①

I WONDER WHERE THAT DOOR LEADS

LET'S INVESTIGATE.... WE'VE GOT TO FIND A HIDING-PLACE........

②

ANY PORT IN A STORM........WHY, IT LOOKS LIKE THEIR ARSENAL!

③

QUIET, DALE... THE GUARDS ARE SEARCHING THE HALL

THIS DOOR IS LOCKED...... THEY COULDN'T GET IN.... THEY MUST BE DOWN THE HALL........

④

FLASH, ISN'T THERE SOMETHING HERE THAT WE CAN USE TO RESCUE ZARKOV?

THERE SHOULD BE, SWEETHEART....LET'S SEE WHAT WE CAN FIND.........

⑤

7-19

MEANWHILE, IN THE PRISON CELL, PLUTON RECOVERS.............

NO TRACE OF THEM YET, LORD PLUTON

KEEP SEARCHING, FOOL! HE MAY TRY TO RESCUE HIS FRIEND, ZARKOV, HERE........

⑥

NEXT WEEK:
HUMAN BAIT

PLUTON DECIDES TO USE THE CAPTIVE, ZARKOV, TO BAIT A TRAP FOR FLASH!

IF WE DON'T CATCH HIM, YOUR FRIEND, FLASH, WILL TRY TO RESCUE YOU.....AND YOU WON'T TELL HIM HE'S WALKING INTO A TRAP EITHER!

WHEN THE SWITCH IS ON, THE INVISIBLE RAYS WILL DESTROY WHOEVER ENTERS THE ROOM!

GOOD! NOW FILL THE HALLS WITH MAN-EATING SHARKONS!

FLASH, HIDING IN THE UNDERSEA ARSENAL, PREPARES TO RESCUE ZARKOV..........

DON'T GO YET, DARLING WE'VE ONLY HAD A MINUTE TOGETHER....AND YOU MAY GET KILLED!

YOU KNOW I LOVE YOU, DALE.....BUT I CAN'T, DESERT POOR ZARKOV!

I'LL BE BACK, DARLING...... KEEP THIS DOOR BARRED!

7-26

A SIXTH SENSE WARNS FLASH, AS THE SHARKON ATTACKS!

THE SCENT OF BLOOD BRINGS THE OTHER SHARKONS!

NEXT WEEK:
**SPRINGING THE TRAP** ∽

58

IN THE HALL OF THE UNDERSEA PRISON, FLASH IS ATTACKED BY MAN-EATING SHARKONS.....HE BACKS AWAY TOWARD THE DOOR OF THE ARSENAL............

DALE! DALE! IT'S FLASH...LET ME IN, QUICK!

DON'T BE FRIGHTENED, DALE... I'LL KILL OFF THESE SHARK-ONS AND THEN RESCUE ZAR-KOV.....

ZARKOV! ALWAYS ZARKOV! YOU RISK YOUR LIFE FOR HIM AND LEAVE ME IN THIS AWFUL PLACE!

THIS ISN'T LIKE YOU, DALE.. YOU WOULDN'T HAVE ME DESERT ZARKOV, WOULD YOU?

I'M SORRY, DEAR...PLEASE FORGIVE ME.........I CAN'T STAND SEEING YOU THROW YOUR LIFE AWAY.......I LOVE YOU SO MUCH!

NOT KNOWING THAT ZARKOV'S PRISON CELL IS A DEATH TRAP, FLASH GOES TO HIS RESCUE...............

........A WOUNDED SHARKON DARTS AT HIS BACK.....FLASH DUCKS IN TIME AND........

THE FISH'S SPEED CARRIES IT INTO THE ELECTRIC TRAP!

NEXT WEEK: A DARING TRICK!

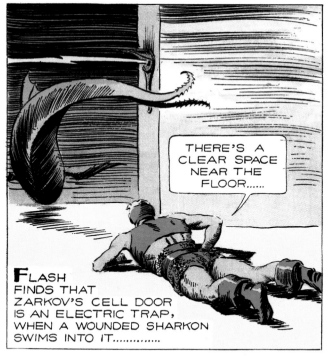

NEXT WEEK:
# A STRANGE BARGAIN

HIDING IN THE SEA-QUEEN'S ARSENAL, FLASH, DALE AND ZARKOV PLAN THEIR ESCAPE............

THAT MACHINE·RIFLE OUGHT TO GET US OUT OF A JAM!

FLASH! MEN ARE COMING DOWN THE HALL!

THAT FLASH KILLED A LOT OF SHARKONS MAKING HIS GET-AWAY!

YES...I'M ALMOST GLAD THE FELLOW GOT AWAY FROM PLUTON AT THAT!

WHY IS UNDINA HAVING US INSPECT THE ARSENAL LORD TRITON?

EMPEROR MING THREATENS TO DECLARE WAR ON US........THE FOOL!

ZARKOV, DALE AND FLASH, HIDDEN BEHIND PILED WEAPONS, WATCH THE APPROACH OF THE MEN............

DON'T MOVE, TRITON, OR I'LL SHOOT!

NEATLY TRAPPED! SO THIS IS WHERE YOU'VE BEEN HIDING, FLASH!

I DON'T WANT TO HARM YOU, TRITON... CAN'T YOU PERSUADE UNDINA TO LET US GO FREE?

IF SHE DOESN'T, WE'LL DESTROY HER ARSENAL, WHICH WON'T HELP HER WAR PLANS AT ALL!

ALL RIGHT... I'LL CALL HER AND SEE....

8-16

UNDINA, FLASH IS GOING TO KILL ME AND DESTROY THE ARSENAL, UNLESS YOU LET THEM ALL GO FREE

IF HE WILL FIGHT LOYALLY, UNTIL MING IS DEFEATED, I'LL LET HIM AND HIS FRIENDS GO FREE

FINE! I AGREE!

CAN WE TRUST HER?

NEXT WEEK:
### WAR THREATS!

FLASH AND ZARKOV JOIN THE SEA-QUEEN'S ARMY, WHEN SHE PROMISES THEM THEIR FREEDOM...........

IT'LL BE A PLEASURE TO FIGHT AGAINST MING, UNDINA!

RIGHT!

HE HAS ALREADY DE-CLARED WAR!

THE VENGEFUL PLUTON BURSTS INTO THE CONFERENCE-ROOM.........

YOUR MAJESTY, THESE REBELS HAVE ESCAPED FROM MY JAIL! GIVE THEM BACK TO ME!

I HAVE GIVEN THEM MY WORD... WOULD YOU MAKE ME A LIAR?

I WARN YOU, I WON'T FORGET THESE INSULTS!

BACK TO YOUR CELL, TORTURER!

OUR AIRSHIPS WILL MAKE A FAKE ATTACK....BUT I COUNT ON YOUR UNDER-SEA FLEET, AD-MIRAL CHIUNG, TO DESTROY UNDINA'S KINGDOM.....

MEANWHILE, FROM HIS DIS-TANT CAPITAL, MING LAUNCHES HIS ATTACK........

LIKE SO MANY STEEL SHARKS, CHIUNG'S SUBMARINE FLEET DIVES INTO UNDINA'S "SEA OF MYSTERY"

8-23

IN HER SEA PALACE, UNDINA SCOFFS AT MING'S THREATS........

EVEN IF HIS ROCKET SHIPS FIND THEIR WAY THROUGH OUR FOGS, WE'LL DESTROY THEM WITH OUR MAGNETO-RAY......

THEY CAN'T HURT US!

MING IS TOO INTELL-IGENT....HE MUST HAVE HAD SOME SECRET TRICK BEFORE HE DECLARED WAR........

NEXT WEEK:
## SURPRISE ATTACK

MING'S AIR FLEET APPROACHES THE UNDERSEA CITY OF CORALIA..............

THE "Z" RAY LOCATED THEIR CITY, JUST AS WE EXPECTED!

SHALL WE RELEASE THE SUPER-DEPTH BOMBS, CAPTAIN?

SUDDENLY, MAGNETO-RAYS FROM THE OCEAN DEPTHS SEIZE THE ROCKET SHIPS AND DRAG THEM TO THEIR DOOM!

SPLENDID WORK, TRITON! THAT'LL TEACH MING BETTER MANNERS!

I CAN'T BELIEVE MING INTENDED TO DEFEAT YOU FROM THE AIR, UNDINA...... MAY I BORROW A SPEED-SLED FOR A LITTLE SCOUTING?

RACING AROUND CORALIA, FLASH RUNS INTO MING'S SUBMARINE FLEET!

RIDE 'IM, COWBOY!

THE FLEET OPENS FIRE....THE SEA BOILS AND ROCKS UNDER MIGHTY EXPLOSIONS....FLASH ESCAPES, ZIGZAGGING WILDLY................

FLASH PAUSES LONG ENOUGH TO RESCUE UNDINA AND TRITON, THEN DASHES FOR CORALIA............

OUR ONLY CHANCE IS BEHIND THE CITY WALLS!

THEY'LL CAPTURE MY MAGNETO-RAY GUNS!

THEY'D HAVE CAPTURED US, TOO, IF IT HADN'T BEEN FOR FLASH!

=NEXT WEEK=
## THE UNDERSEA SIEGE

FLASH BARELY MAKES THE GATES OF CORALIA, AHEAD OF MING'S SUBMARINES...........

TRITON RUSHES TO THE MAIN CONTROL-ROOM AND DIRECTS HIS TORPEDO-GUNS AGAINST MING'S SUBMARINE FLEET..............

BY TAO, THEY'RE RUNNING AWAY! YES, THEY'RE OUT OF RANGE ALREADY... OUR TORPEDO-GUNS CAN'T REACH THEM!

NICE WORK, TRITON!

AT THAT MOMENT, QUEEN UNDINA ENTERS THE CONTROL-ROOM........

FLASH, YOUR SCOUTING TRIP SAVED CORALIA..... MING IS ROUTED....I AM GRATEFUL!

DON'T BE TOO SURE THAT MING HAS GIVEN UP THE ATTACK!

A TERRIFIC EXPLOSION SHAKES CORALIA- A SECTION OF ITS STOUT WALLS CRUMBLE

© 1936, King Features Syndicate, Inc., World rights reserved.

MORE EXPLOSIONS ROCK THE UNDERSEA CITY..........

I'LL GET ZARKOV....HE MAY THINK OF SOMETHING.....

THEY'RE BOMBARDING US WITH TORPEDOES....AND THEY'RE OUT OF RANGE OF OUR GUNS!

OUR WALLS CAN'T STAND THIS!

9-6

-: NEXT WEEK :-
FIGHTING FIRE WITH FIRE!

WE HAVE NO WEAPON THAT CAN REACH THEM.....

I'LL LEAD A COUNTER-ATTACK WITH SPEED SLEDS

NO....YOU'D HAVE NO CHANCE OF SUCCESS... WAIT....JUST HOW DO YOU HEAT AND COOL THE CITY?

MING'S SUBMARINES ARE BLASTING THE UNDER-SEA CITY WITH LONG-RANGE TORPEDOES...............

TRITON SHOWS THEM THE GIANT WATER-CONDITIONING PLANT.............

THIS KEEPS US COOL IN THE HOTTEST SUMMER.....

...AND THIS IS THE HEATING OUTFIT FOR WINTER?

AS ZARKOV, HIGH IN A CABLE CAR, BARKS DIRECTIONS THROUGH AN AQUAPHONE, MEN HAUL HUGE ELECTRIC CABLES FROM THE CITY TO THE SURROUNDING HILLS....THE EARTH SCIENTIST IS ABOUT TO CONDUCT A DARING EXPERIMENT!

WHILE THE WATER-COOLING PLANT RUNS FULL STRENGTH INSIDE CORALIA, HEAT IS POURED INTO THE WATER OUTSIDE.............

HORROR AND CONFUSION GRIP THE SUBMARINE FLEET, AS THE WATER AROUND THE CITY BEGINS TO BOIL............

9-13

THE PITIFUL REMNANTS OF MING'S FLEET RUN FOR THEIR LIVES!

ALL SHIPS......BACK TO MING'S HARBOR, FULL SPEED! ADMIRAL CHIUNG SPEAKING!

≈ NEXT WEEK ≈
**TRIUMPH AND TREACHERY**

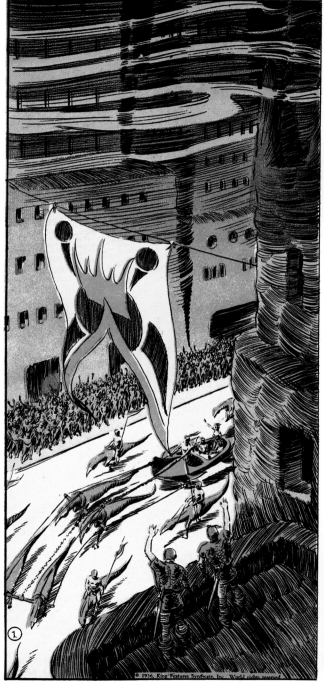

65

JOY SWEEPS THE UNDERSEA CITY OF CORALIA AS MING'S SUBMARINE FLEET IS ROUTED...........

AN OMINOUS NOTE CREEPS INTO THE ROYAL CELEBRATION.............

WHERE IS LORD PLUTON?

GENERAL TRITON, LORD PLUTON SENT FOR YOU....HE HAS DISCOVERED A PLOT AGAINST THE THRONE!

HE WAS TOO BUSY TO COME......

AGAIN A MESSAGE COMES FROM PLUTON'S PRISON............

YOUR MAJESTY, LORD PLUTON REQUESTS YOUR IMMEDIATE PRESENCE....VERY URGENT

DON'T INTERRUPT YOUR BANQUET.... I'LL BE RIGHT BACK AFTER I SETTLE THIS NONSENSE!

SOMETHING'S FISHY, ZARKOV!

VERY QUEER....REMEMBER HOW PLUTON SWORE REVENGE ON TRITON AND UNDINA FOR FREEING US?

FLASH, PLEASE DON'T MEDDLE IN THEIR AFFAIRS.....

YOU WAIT HERE....IF THERE'S A PLOT, PLUTON IS AT THE HEAD OF IT!

SPYING ON PLUTON'S CELLS, FLASH SEES AN AMAZING SIGHT.............

YOU'LL DIE FOR THIS TREASON, PLUTON!

YOU'LL NEVER SEE ME DIE, UNDINA....I'LL KEEP YOU IN ETERNAL DARKNESS, WHILE I RULE CORALIA AND PUNISH THOSE THREE EARTHLINGS!

NEXT WEEK: TREASON'S REWARD

AMAZING NEWS....UNDINA PROMISES TO MAKE FLASH, DALE AND ZARKOV NORMAL, AIR-BREATHING HUMANS AGAIN!............

THE ROYAL WEDDING..... A CELEBRATION OF FLASH'S VICTORY OVER MING'S SUBMARINES.......

WHAT'S THE MATTER, DARLING? DON'T YOU WANT TO LEAVE THE UNDERSEA WORLD?

YOU WON'T MIND STAYING HERE FOR MY MARRIAGE TO TRITON, WILL YOU?

YES, SILLY...I'M CRYING FOR HAPPINESS!

....THEREFORE, MY DEAR HUSBAND, I CROWN THEE KING TRITON, RULER OF ALL CORALIA.........

KING TRITON AND QUEEN UNDINA LEAD THE WAY TO THE CORAL ATOLL AFTER THE WEDDING............

THERE, UNDER TRITON'S DIRECTION, BEGINS THE DELICATE AND COMPLEX PROCESS OF RESTORING THE LUNGS OF FLASH, DALE AND ZARKOV TO NORMAL.......

AT LAST THE THREE EARTHLINGS CAN BREATHE AIR AGAIN!

NOTHING EVER TASTED BETTER!

THANK YOU, UNDINA... AND FORGIVE ME FOR DOUBTING YOU.....

A SUCCESSFUL EXPERIMENT! WOULD YOU EXPLAIN THE PRINCIPLE TO ME, TRITON?

GLAD TO, ZARKOV....

10-4

NEXT WEEK ➤ A SECRET FLIGHT

FREED FROM THE UNDERSEA WORLD, THE THREE EARTHLINGS FACE THE FUTURE........

WHERE DO WE GO FROM HERE, FLASH?

DARLING, I'M SICK OF ADVENTURE AND DANGER....WHY CAN'T WE STAY HERE?

WE'D GET SICKER OF THIS TINY ISLAND......

I THOUGHT YOU MIGHT USE ONE OF THE ROCKET SHIPS WE CAPTURED FROM MING........

UNDINA, I'LL NEVER FORGET YOUR KINDNESS........

UNDINA MAKES THEM A PARTING GIFT.........

THE ROCKET SHIP ZOOMS SKYWARD TO THE FAREWELL CHEERS OF UNDINA AND HER SOLDIERS......

I'VE CHECKED EVERYTHING..... IT'S IN PERFECT ORDER......

GOODBYE, UNDINA..... WE'LL NEVER FORGET YOU!

GOODBYE, TRITON....

I SUPPOSE YOU ARE GOING TO GET INTO ANOTHER WAR NOW.... I TELL YOU I'M SICK OF FIGHTING!

SO AM I, DARLING..... I WANT TO SETTLE DOWN PEACEFULLY IF MING WILL LET US, ZARKOV, HEAD FOR BARIN'S FOREST KINGDOM

I HOPE I CAN DODGE MING'S AIR PATROLS!

NEXT ─: WEEK :─

**DEATH ABOVE THE CLOUDS**

10-11

**F**LASH HEADS FOR HIS FRIEND, BARIN'S, FORESTS IN MING'S CAPTURED ROCKET SHIP..............

NOW THAT WE'RE OUT OF THE SEA FOGS, WE RUN THE RISK OF BEING SPOTTED BY MING'S AIR PATROLS.....

BY TAO..... YOU'RE TOO GOOD A PROPHET.... THERE'S ONE NOW!

THEY'RE GAINING ON US....AND THEY'RE 'PHONING US ORDERS TO STOP

THIS CALLS FOR STRATEGY... HELLO, PATROL, WHAT DO YOU WANT? WE ARE ON A SECRET MISSION FOR THE EMPEROR....CAPTAIN CHIUNG SPEAKING..........

**W**ITH A BURST OF SPEED, FLASH TRIES TO OUT-DISTANCE THE ENEMY................

LIARS! CHIUNG IS DEAD! LAND YOUR SHIP OR WE FIRE!

HOLD THAT COURSE....MY ATOM CANNON IS ALMOST SQUARELY ON THEM!

WE'LL HAVE TO FIGHT FLASH!

10-18
© 1936, King Features Syndicate, Inc., World rights reserved

**O**NE SQUARE HIT WRECKS THE ENEMY PATROL ROCKET!................

**B**UT WHILE FLASH ROCKETS TOWARD SAFETY, GRIM PLANS ARE AFOOT IN MING'S PATROL HEADQUARTERS!..............

YOU KNOW WE RECORD ALL MESSAGES FROM ROCKET SHIPS..... THIS IS THE ONE I CALLED YOU ABOUT..........

FOR THE EMPEROR... CAPTAIN CHIUNG SPEAKING..

BY TAO, THAT'S FLASH GORDON'S VOICE! NOTIFY ALL PATROLS TO INTERCEPT HIS ROCKET SHIP!

NEXT WEEK: **FLAMING FATE!**

FLYING HIGH, FLASH NEARS THE FOREST KINGDOM OF HIS FRIEND, BARIN............

THAT LOOKS LIKE HIGH FORESTS ON THE HORIZON

I'M SO GLAD......... WE'LL BE AMONG FRIENDS AGAIN!

GOOD...WE'VE DODGED MING'S PATROLS

1.

INSIDE THE FLAMING, WRECKED SHIP, ZARKOV BATTLES THE CONTROLS...........

MY POOR DARLING!

IF WE CAN ONLY LAND IN THE FOREST......

THIS IS THE END, FLASH!

BUT ALL OF MING'S ROCKETS ARE CLOSING IN ON THE REBEL SHIP.......

2.

THE FLEET COMMANDER REPORTS TO MING..

THEIR ROCKET-SHIP CRASHED AT THE EDGE OF THE FOREST.....

LAND AND BRING ME FLASH GORDON'S BODY, SO I CAN BE SURE HE'S DEAD!

5.

10-25

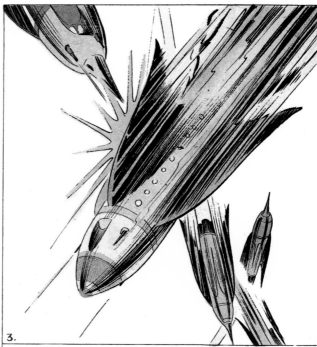

3.

TRAPPED AND OUTNUMBERED, FLASH AND ZARKOV ACCOUNT FOR A NUMBER OF SHIPS BEFORE THEY ARE BLASTED IN MIDAIR...........

WITH AMAZING SKILL, ZARKOV MADE A PANCAKE LANDING WITH HIS BLAZING SHIP... BADLY BATTERED, THEY STAGGER INTO THE FOREST................

NEXT WEEK

## HUNTED CREATURES

6.

BROUGHT DOWN IN FLAMES, FLASH AND HIS COMPANIONS FLEE IN THE FOREST................

I DON'T LIKE THE WAY THOSE ROCKETS FOLLOWED US DOWN!

PUT OUT THE FIRE. THEN HUNT FOR BODIES!

MING'S AIRMEN, FOLLOWING ORDERS, TRY TO MAKE SURE OF FLASH'S DEATH IN HIS WRECKED SHIP................

BUT FIRE REACHES THE WRECK'S POWDER MAGAZINE!................

BACK TO THE SHIP, MEN.... WE'RE TAKING OFF!

HIS SEARCH BALKED BY THE EXPLOSION, MING'S COMMANDER ORDERS THE FOREST BURNED IN A WIDE CIRCLE TO TRAP ANY POSSIBLE SURVIVORS................

11-1

A RING OF FIRE SURROUNDS THE FUGITIVES

FLASH....THE FIRE FROM THE ROCKETS MUST HAVE SPREAD!

THERE'S SMOKE AHEAD TOO, FLASH! LOOK! FLAMES IN THE TREES OVER THERE! WE'RE CUT OFF!

NEXT WEEK: FOREST FIRE~

72

TRAPPED IN A BLAZING FOREST, FLASH AND HIS FRIENDS RUN FOR THEIR LIVES......

STRANGE FOREST CREATURES JOIN THE FLIGHT FOR LIFE............

SUDDENLY, ZARKOV DISCOVERS AN OMINOUS FACT............

FLASH DESPERATELY SCRAMBLES UP A TREE TO SEE IF THERE IS ANY ESCAPE....

A SMALL FOREST LAKE OFFERS PERILOUS REFUGE............

11-8

WHAT'LL WE DO, FLASH? HE'S COMING THIS WAY!

UGH....HOW HORRIBLE!

HOLD TIGHT, EVERYBODY.... I'VE AN IDEA..

HIDING IN A SMALL LAKE FROM THE FLAMES OF A FOREST FIRE, FLASH IS MENACED BY WILD ANIMALS..............

SEIZING A FLOATING BRANCH AS A WEAPON, FLASH SWIMS TOWARD THE MAN-EATING URSODILE TO DIVERT ITS ATTENTION FROM HIS FRIENDS....AS THE BEAST LUNGES AT HIM, HE DIVES..........

AS THE URSODILE DIVES AFTER FLASH, HE THRUSTS THE STICK BETWEEN THE BEAST'S GAPING JAWS..............

THE MONSTER FLEES, LASHING THE WATER IN AGONY...............

YOU SAVED OUR LIVES AGAIN, DARLING!

WE'RE DRIFTING TOO CLOSE TO SHORE....THE FLAMES ARE COMING THIS WAY AGAIN!

MEANWHILE, MING'S ROCKETS SURVEY THE BLAZING FOREST........

AS THE FIRE BURNS LOWER, THE SKY COMMANDER GIVES AN ORDER.........

NOBODY HAS ESCAPED FROM THE FOREST ALIVE....ALL SHIPS, ATTEN-TION.......... RETURN TO THE CAPITAL.... WE SHALL REPORT FLASH'S DEATH!

11-15

NEXT WEEK — **TRAGIC NEWS**

MING'S COMMANDER REPORTS THAT HE HAS KILLED FLASH...............

YOUR SUPREME INTELLIGENCE, FLASH'S ROCKET WAS BROUGHT DOWN AFIRE... WE LANDED AND SAW IT EXPLODE....THEN WE FIRED A TWENTY-MILE CIRCLE OF FOREST....NOTHING ESCAPED BUT A FEW SMALL ANIMALS

YOU HAVE DONE WELL, COMMANDER LU CHAO....I MAKE THEE LORD LU CHAO!

ALL LOYAL SUBJECTS WILL REJOICE TO HEAR THAT THE REBEL EARTH-MAN, FLASH GORDON, AND HIS COMPANIONS WERE BURNED ALIVE IN THE EDGE OF THE FORESTS OF BA-RIN, NEAR MOUNT KARAKAS..... THIS IS.......

MING BROADCASTS THE REPORT TO ALL THE PLANET OF MONGO............

IN THE TREE-KINGDOM OF FLASH'S FRIEND, BARIN...........

HE MUST HAVE BEEN ON HIS WAY TO MY FOR-ESTS, AURA

.....THIS IS YOUR EMPEROR SPEAK-ING.......

OH, FATHER MING, HOW CRUEL TO GLOAT OVER FLASH! I LOVED FLASH BEFORE I MET YOU, BARIN, DARLING......

FLASH AND HIS COMRADES FELL NEAR KARAKAS IN THE FORESTS.. SPREAD OUT AND SEARCH ON ALL SIDES OF THE FIRE, THEN LOOK IN THE BURNED AREA FOR BODIES.......

WE WON'T COME BACK EMPTY-HANDED, KING BARIN......

MEANWHILE, IN A TINY FIRE-CIRCLED LAKE..

I DO THINK THE FLAMES ARE DYING DOWN AT LAST.....

YOU'RE RIGHT, SWEET..... NOW, ZARKOV, HOLD STILL WHILE I BANDAGE THAT GASH IN YOUR ARM

11-22

~ NEXT WEEK ~
~ **THE FOREST PLAGUE**

IF WE CAN ONLY CROSS THE PLAIN TO THE GIANT FORESTS AND REACH SOME OF BARIN'S FOREST PEOPLE

I'M TOO GLAD TO BE ALIVE, TO WORRY ABOUT THE FUTURE

AT LEAST MING'S ROCKETS HAVE GIVEN UP AND GONE HOME

AFTER THE FIRE DIES DOWN, FLASH LEADS THE WAY THROUGH THE BURNED AREA..........

IT COULDN'T BE ANOTHER FIRE... BUT THE WILD ANIMALS ARE RUNNING FROM SOMETHING...... LET'S HURRY!

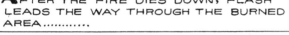

THEY ARE WITHIN SIGHT OF THE GIANT FORESTS OF BARIN, NEAR MOUNT KARAKAS, WHEN THE TERROR CATCHES UP WITH THEM...THE MAD SQUIRLONS OF MOUNT KARAKAS!

© 1936, King Features Syndicate Inc. World rights reserved

COME ON, FLASH... DON'T WAIT ANY LONGER...

I'VE HEARD THEIR BITE IS LIKE A MAD DOG'S... ALMOST CERTAIN DEATH!

HURRY, ZARKOV!

AS THEY REACH THE TOP OF THE TREE, THE MAD HORDE IS UPON THEM!

11-29

NEXT WEEK
MAD SIEGE

TRAPPED IN A HUGE TREE IN THE FORESTS OF BARIN, THE THREE EARTHLINGS FIGHT OFF A FLOOD OF MAD SQUIRLONS....A SINGLE BITE MEANS MADNESS!......

I HOPE OUR STAY IN THE LAKE DIDN'T DROWN OUT MY PISTOL OUR ONLY CHANCE IS TO SET THAT DEAD TREE ON FIRE....THE FLAMES MAY DRIVE THEM AWAY.....

TEN BOLTS FROM FLASH'S GUN BRING THE TREE DOWN IN FLAMES....THE SQUIRLONS FLEE IN TERROR...........

BUT ONE OF THE MAD ANIMALS BITES ZARKOV!......

ONE OF 'EM GOT ME!

12·6

POOR ZARKOV! CAN I DO ANY-THING TO HELP?

CUT OPEN THE BITE AND MAKE IT BLEED.. ARE YOU ALL RIGHT, FLASH?

I'M HOLDING THEM OFF...... KEEP YOUR CHIN UP, OLD MAN!

NEXT WEEK: **A GRIM CHOICE**

THE MAD SQUIRLONS STILL KEEP THE THREE HUMANS TRAPPED IN A TREE............

THEY'VE STOPPED CLIMBING...THEY'RE FIGHTING OVER THE WOUNDED ANIMALS...

HOLD STILL, ZARKOV, TILL I BANDAGE THAT BITE......

STOP IT! QUIT HURTING ME!

I HATE YOU! YOU'RE ALL AGAINST ME! I'M ON FIRE! YAH-H-H-H!

ZARKOV! OH, HELP, FLASH, HE'S GOING MAD!

MADNESS FROM THE SQUIRLON'S BITE RUNS THROUGH ZARKOV'S VEINS!......

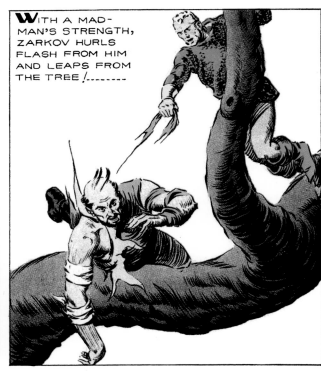

WITH A MADMAN'S STRENGTH, ZARKOV HURLS FLASH FROM HIM AND LEAPS FROM THE TREE!........

MANY BRANCHES BREAK ZARKOV'S FALL AND HE LANDS ON THE HORDE OF VICIOUS SQUIRLONS!............

ZARKOV FIGHTS OFF THE BEASTS AND RUNS WILDLY INTO THE FOREST......

WATER! I'M BURNING UP! WATER!

12-13

HOW AWFUL..... POOR ZARKOV! THE FOREST IS ALIVE WITH DANGER!

I SHOULD FOLLOW AND HELP HIM...BUT I CAN'T LEAVE YOU ALONE, DALE

⊹ NEXT WEEK ⊹
SEARCH PARTY

WE ARE VERY NEAR TO MOUNT KARAKAS--AND NO SIGN OF FIRE YET....

NO, SIR-- AND NO TRACKS

COMBING THE FORESTS OF BARIN'S KINGDOM, CAPTAIN TRUNO LEADS THE SEARCH FOR FLASH'S PARTY..........

MAD SQUIRLONS.... GIVE THEM A GAS BARRAGE!

THE SEARCHERS FIND THAT THE SQUIRLONS HAD BEEN ATTACKING A FALLEN MAN........

IT'S A MAN! QUICK, TELL THE DOCTOR TO GIVE HIM ANTI-GAS AND TREATMENT FOR SQUIRLON POISON!

YES, SIR...

WHO ARE YOU?

PROFESSOR ZARKOV..... WHERE AM I? WHO ARE YOU?

12-20

ZARKOV SEEMS TO RECOVER--BUT HE IS STILL AFFECTED BY THE ANIMAL VENOM...

ZARKOV? THEN YOU WERE WITH FLASH GORDON--WHERE IS HE? WHERE IS THE GIRL?

GONE! DEAD! ALL DEAD! I'M AFIRE-- WATER, WATER, I'M BURNING--WE'RE ALL BURNING!

AND WHILE FLASH AND DALE ARE STILL TRAPPED IN A TREE NOT FAR AWAY, CAPTAIN TRUNO BELIEVES ZARKOV'S RAVINGS AND TURNS BACK.............

DOCTOR, GIVE ZARKOV ANOTHER TREATMENT.. DRUMMER, REPORT TO BARIN THAT FLASH AND DALE ARE DEAD AND THAT WE ARE RETURN- ING WITH ZARKOV

--≡ NEXT WEEK ≡--
**ALONE IN THE FOREST**~

I HOPE WE CATCH UP WITH HIM THIS MORNING..

IF ONLY I DON'T LOSE HIS TRAIL..

TRAILING THEIR CRAZED COMRADE, ZARKOV, FLASH AND DALE PUSH ON THROUGH THE FOREST..........

WHAT'S THAT? IT SOUNDS LIKE A DISTANT DRUM.... MORE ENEMIES?

NO..SOME OF BARIN'S PEOPLE.. HELLO-O-O!

THERE IS NO ANSWER, SO FLASH AND DALE HURRY TOWARD THE SOUND....

THOSE DRUMS CARRY FOR MILES--I HOPE WE FIND THE FOREST MEN..

I CAN'T HEAR IT ANY MORE..

AT THE DISTANT CAMP, TRUNO SIGNALS TO KING BARIN..............

TELL BARIN THAT ZARKOV IS WORSE.. WE WILL PADDLE FULL SPEED TOWARD HOME....

HOURS LATER, FLASH AND DALE REACH THE LAKE SHORE..............

THE TRACKS LEAD UP TO THE WATER

YES.. SOMEONE FOUND ZARKOV AND TOOK HIM IN A BOAT..BUT WHICH WAY DID THEY GO? IF WE CIRCLE THE LAKE, WE MAY PICK THEM UP AGAIN..

BUT THEIR DESPERATE ATTEMPT TO CIRCLE THE LAKE ENDS IN DISASTER--THEY BECOME LOST IN A DISMAL SWAMP!..........

1-3

NEXT WEEK:-
THE CLUTCH OF DEATH!

FLASH AND DALE, HOPELESSLY LOST IN THE JUNGLE, CONTINUE THEIR SEARCH FOR BARIN'S FOREST PEOPLE......

A HEAVY CRASHING NOISE REACHES THEIR EARS__SUDDENLY, A GIANT MAGNOPED LUMBERS INTO VIEW!_____

SEEKING REFUGE, FLASH AND DALE SCRAMBLE INTO A TREE_____

HE'S COMING TOWARD THIS TREE!

UGH____ WHAT A HORRIBLE CREATURE!

THE HUGE BEAST SEIZES A VINE WHICH HANGS FROM THE LIMB ON WHICH FLASH AND DALE ARE PERCHED__ HE SHAKES THE LIMB UNTIL DALE TOPPLES TO THE GROUND!_____

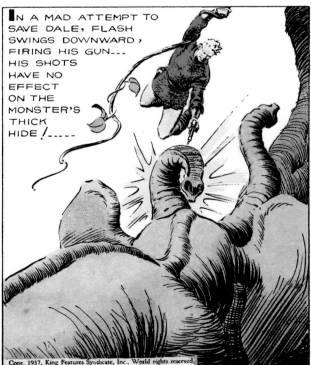

IN A MAD ATTEMPT TO SAVE DALE, FLASH SWINGS DOWNWARD, FIRING HIS GUN___ HIS SHOTS HAVE NO EFFECT ON THE MONSTER'S THICK HIDE!_____

STUNG TO FURY, THE MAGNOPED SNATCHES FLASH FROM HIS VINE AND RAISES A MIGHTY FOOT!_____

1-17

≡ NEXT WEEK ≡
## THE STRANGLER

STUNNED, FLASH AND DALE LIE HELPLESS, AS THE ENRAGED MAGNOPED RISES TO STAMP OUT THEIR LIVES !---------

LIKE WHIPS, CURLING VINES LASH DOWN FROM A NEARBY TREE !------

WITH FIEND- ISH SKILL, THEY TIGHTEN AROUND THE SCREAMING MONSTER !------

SHOCKED OUT OF HIS DAZE, FLASH TRIES TO CARRY DALE AWAY FROM THE CANNIBAL VINES ------

BUT THE HUNGRY TENDRILS CATCH FLASH-----

--AND DRAW HIM INTO THE AIR !--------

1-24

AT THAT INSTANT, DALE REGAINS CONSCIOUSNESS ------

OH, FLASH...MY DARLING ! **MY DARLING !**

≡ NEXT WEEK ≡
**FATE STRIKES !**

① FLASH AND DALE ARE LOST IN THE DISMAL JUNGLES OF BARIN__DURING THEIR SEARCH FOR THE CRAZED DR. ZARKOV, FLASH IS CAUGHT IN A STRANGLER VINE!__

__DALE'S TERRIFIED SCREAMS MINGLE WITH THE THUNDER OF AN APPROACHING STORM!_____

② BLIND TO EVERYTHING BUT FLASH'S DANGER, DALE DASHES BACK TO THE SPOT WHERE FLASH HAD DROPPED HIS GUN IN THE BATTLE WITH THE MAGNOPED_____

④ JUST AS THE TRAPPED HUMANS REACH THE LIMIT OF ENDURANCE, A BOLT OF LIGHTNING STRIKES THE TREE!_____

③ BUT, IN ATTEMPTING TO KILL THE PLANT, SHE VENTURES TOO CLOSE

⑤ SAVED BY THE FREAKISH BOLT OF LIGHTNING THAT KILLED THE LIVING VINE, FLASH AND DALE STUMBLE INTO EACH OTHERS ARMS_____

WE'RE SAFE, DARLING__ SAFE!___AND TO THINK YOU ALMOST GAVE YOUR LIFE IN TRYING TO SAVE MINE!

LIFE? WHAT IS LIFE COMPARED TO A LOVE LIKE OURS?

1-31

≡ NEXT WEEK ≡
**THE HUNTERS**

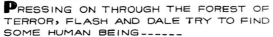 PRESSING ON THROUGH THE FOREST OF TERROR, FLASH AND DALE TRY TO FIND SOME HUMAN BEING------

BARIN AND HIS PEOPLE LIVE SOMEWHERE IN THESE JUNGLES

I DON'T BELIEVE IT, DARLING__WE HAVEN'T SEEN A TRACE OF A HUMAN BEING YET

I DON'T FEEL SAFE WITHOUT SOME SORT OF A WEAPON__I'LL JUST CUT MYSELF A SPEAR

I'LL NEVER FEEL SAFE IN THIS AWFUL PLACE__OH, FLASH___WHAT'S EVER GOING TO BECOME OF US?

DARLING, THIS IS A TRAIL___LOOK___SOMEBODY'S FOOTPRINT!

IT JUST MEANS ANOTHER ENEMY__OH, I'M SO SORRY TO BE SUCH A SISSY, DEAR___

AS FLASH EAGERLY FOLLOWS THE TRAIL, A TUSK-MAN RISES AND GIVES A SIGNAL____

SUDDENLY, FROM ALL SIDES, SAVAGE TUSK-MEN LEAP AT FLASH AND DALE!_____

NEXT WEEK

AMONG THE TUSK-MEN~

2-7

Flash and Dale are surprised by a band of savage tusk-men—

OH, STOP! DON'T HURT HIM!

1.

DON'T KILL HIM! PLEASE DON'T HARM HIM! OH, DEAR— THEY CAN'T UNDERSTAND ME!

2.

The tusk-men set off at a trot with their captives—

3.

NEXT WEEK

SAVAGE FEAST

Their path leads through weird jungle country—over great, yawning canyons and boiling rivers—

4.

"BRAK"— HOW YOU SAY? COOK? YA, YA, COOK YOU!

5.

—To a great jungle, far underneath—in which is spread a vast network of caves—the home of the tusk-men—

3-14

ONE-TUSK ORDERS HIS MEN TO THROW FLASH INTO THE FLAMES FOR THEIR FEAST_____

AT A SIGNAL FROM ONE-TUSK, THE HOWLING TUSK-MEN DRAG FLASH TOWARD A HUGE FIRE!_____

AS FLASH HURTLES INTO THE SEARING FLAMES, HE HEAVES DESPERATELY AT HIS BONDS--THEY SNAP_____

WITH A SNARL OF FURY, FLASH HURLS HIMSELF AT HIS TORMENTORS-- MANY DROP UNDER HIS CLUB-LIKE FISTS_____

ONE NOOSE SNARES FLASH____ANOTHER AND ANOTHER____HE IS DRAGGED BACK TOWARD THE FIRE!_____

NEXT WEEK: STRIPED DEATH!

2-21

Holding flash helpless with their rope vines, the tusk-men prepare to cook him alive.......

But a roar echoes through the caves and a hungry tigron leaps at one-tusk!

Slipping out of his bonds, Flash leaps to a high rock, twirling a lasso.........

It hisses through the air and snaps about the tigron's throat... with a mighty heave, Flash pulls the beast into the flames!

2-28

You get meat, we no kill you...no get meat, we eat you and woman!

Having given orders for a feast, one-tusk gives Flash a chance for his life.........

NEXT WEEK:
## HUNT OR BE KILLED

As prisoner of the tusk-men, Flash must find meat for the tribe, or he and Dale will be killed.........

Flash finds a well-worn trail of the huge triden-taurus.......

Tridentaurus tracks--good eating....

No! Gwak kill us! No can kill Gwak with spear--him too big.....

With one tusk's permission, Flash orders the tusk-men to cut saplings and vines according to his directions.........

Now, One Tusk, let me have your fastest runner--I want him to trick a Gwak into chasing him....

A half-hour passes--suddenly, the terrified runner dashes back over the brow of the hill....

Help! Gwak!

As the monster hits the vine that is stretched across the path, Flash cuts the cord holding the bow-string and the spear plunges deep into the great beast's body!

NEXT WEEK: THE FIGHT FOR FOOD

3.7

BY SETTING A HUGE BOW-AND-ARROW TRAP, FLASH HAS KILLED A FIERCE GWAK--

GWAK GOOD TO EAT--- YOU GOOD HUNTER

THANKS, ONE-TUSK--NOW YOU MUST PLAY FAIR WITH DALE AND ME

THE GWAK'S MATE SURPRISES THE TUSK-MEN, WHO ARE BUSY CARVING THE MEAT OF THEIR PRIZE------

AIEE! GWAK! RUN!

AS THE TUSK-MEN FRANTICALLY SCATTER IN ALL DIRECTIONS, FLASH SEIZES A HATCHET AND LEAPS INTO A TREE------

THE MAMMOTH BEAST THUNDERS CLOSE TO THE TREE--FLASH GRITS HIS TEETH AND LEAPS------

HE SWINGS HIS HATCHET AT THE MIGHTY GWAK'S ONE VULNERABLE SPOT--BETWEEN THE EYES!

3-14

AFTER A LONG, ANXIOUS VIGIL, DALE IS REWARDED BY THE SIGHT OF FLASH AND THE TUSK-MEN RETURNING LOADED DOWN WITH PRECIOUS MEAT------

=: NEXT WEEK :=

# A FEAST AND A FIGHT

THE STAGE IS SET.....THE TUSK-MEN ARE ABOUT TO SETTLE THE MATTER BY TRIBAL LAW!

NEXT WEEK

**STONE AGE DUEL**

DON'T WORRY, DALE--

YOU MUST WIN, DARLING__YOU MUST!

ME KILL HIM, BENT-BACK__ ME KNOW HOW FIGHT WITH HAMMER--

FLASH MUST BATTLE ONE-TUSK TO SEE WHICH SHALL BE CHIEF OF THE TUSK-MEN!_____

FLASH PARRIES ONE-TUSK'S FIRST BLOW AND HIS HAMMER BREAKS! DALE SCREAMS WITH TERROR_____

YOUR MAN NO CAN WIN, HA-HA-HA___I GIVE HIM BROKEN HAMMER!

As THE CLUMSY TUSK-MAN RAISES HIS HAMMER TO FINISH THE EARTH-MAN, FLASH SWINGS A TERRIFIC RIGHT!

3-28

He STRAIGHTENS ONE-TUSK WITH A LEFT HOOK, THEN DRIVES ANOTHER RIGHT TO THE SWAYING CHIEF'S JAW__ONE-TUSK COLLAPSES_____

A MIGHTY ROAR GOES UP, HAILING FLASH CHIEF OF THE TUSK-MEN!

NEXT WEEK
# A DANGEROUS DECISION

NEXT WEEK
**AT DEAD OF NIGHT**

FLASH STANDS GUARD OVER DALE, WHO SLEEPS IN A NEARBY ALCOVE, WHILE TWO TUSK-MEN PLAN REBELLION_____

ONE-TUSK AND BENT-BACK, HAMMERS UP-RAISED, CREEP UP ON FLASH !____

WHAT WAS THAT? SOME-ONE STIRRING IN HIS SLEEP, I GUESS

FLASH TURNS AWAY AND ONE-TUSK STRIKES !___

BENT-BACK BRUTALLY STUNS DALE AND CARRIES HER FROM HER ALCOVE_____

US SELL SLAVES, ONE-TUSK.. GET GUNS...

GOOD__ THEN ME CHIEF AGAIN !

NEXT WEEK
**CARRIED INTO SLAVERY !**

4-11

CAPTAIN TRUNO, OF BARIN'S ROYAL FORESTERS, LEADS FLASH AND DALE INTO A WEIRD, GIGANTIC FOREST-------

YOU SAY, CAPTAIN, THAT YOU LIVE IN THE TOPS OF THESE IMMENSE TREES... WHY IS THAT?

BECAUSE, YOUR MAJESTY, THIS FOREST ABOUNDS WITH GREAT, CARNIVOROUS PLANTS AND HUGE, MAN-EATING ANIMALS--DEATH LURKS ON ALL SIDES OF US--SAFETY LIES ONLY IN THE TREES---

BY MEANS OF A VINE ELEVATOR, THEY ARE LIFTED HIGH INTO THE AIR

THEY LAND FOUR HUNDRED FEET ABOVE THE GROUND WHERE THE GREAT HIGHWAY OF THE FOREST KINGDOM BEGINS-----

A LITTLE LATER, FLASH AND DALE STOP IN AWESTRUCK SILENCE, AS AHEAD OF THEM RISES, IN STRANGE MAGNIFICENCE, THE SNOW-WHITE PALACE OF BARIN, THE FOREST KING!

═ NEXT WEEK ═

# WELCOME AND WARNING

**Panel 1.**

AMID THE WELCOMING BLARE OF TRUMPETS, FLASH AND DALE RUSH UP THE STAIRWAY TO BARIN'S TREE PALACE...

THERE'S GOOD OLD BARIN---HE LOOKS THE SAME AS EVER--

AND AURA---SHE USED TO BE IN LOVE WITH YOU, FLASH----

**Panel 2.**

BY TAO, IT'S GOOD TO SEE YOU, FLASH! WE THOUGHT YOU WERE DEAD---

NOT WHILE WE HAVE FRIENDS LIKE YOU TO HELP US!

WELCOME TO ARBORIA, DALE---I SEE YOU MANAGED TO HOLD YOUR MAN----

YES, DARLING---AND AGAINST SOME REAL COMPETITION!

**Panel 3.**

GOSH, AURA, YOU'LL NEVER KNOW HOW GLAD WE WERE TO SEE---HEY!

DARLING! YOU SAY THE SWEETEST THINGS! I'M GLAD YOU ESCAPED FROM MY FATHER--WELCOME----A THOUSAND TIMES WELCOME!

OF ALL THE NERVE!

**Panel 4.**

FLASH'S STANDARD AS KING OF THE CAVE WORLD IS RUN UP UNDERNEATH THAT OF KING BARIN-----A GREAT HONOR-----

**Panel 5.**

A ROYAL BANQUET IS GIVEN IN THE STATE HALL OF THE PALACE...

----AND REMEMBER, MY LOYAL SUBJECTS, NO ONE OUTSIDE THE KINGDOM MUST EVER KNOW THEY ARE ALIVE, LEST THEY FALL INTO THE HANDS OF EMPEROR MING--THEY ARE MY DEAREST FRIENDS, AND I KNOW YOU WILL RESPECT MY WISHES-----

WHY DID YOU LET HER KISS YOU?

NEXT WEEK.....

THE PROWLER

5-2

98

Flash is restless the first night he spends in Barin's palace........

NICE TO BE AMONG FRIENDS FOR A CHANGE! THE QUIET LIFE FOR ME! SAY....WHAT'S GOING ON DOWN THERE?

Flash sees someone crawling into Aura's window!

Seizing a vine, he swings himself to the balcony....

At sight of Flash, the thief cringes and begs for mercy......

FORGIVE ME, KING FLASH! MY WIFE WAS SICK AND I NEEDED MONEY....I NEVER DID ANYTHING WRONG BEFORE

IS THAT THE TRUTH? WILL YOU GO STRAIGHT FROM NOW ON? ALL RIGHT, THEN GET OUT OF HERE!

WHAT'S HAPPENING HERE? WHY..FLASH! WHAT ARE YOU DOING HERE?

WELL, I HEARD A BURGLAR....I GOT YOUR JEWELS BACK, BUT HE ESCAPED....

NOISE? OH, IT WAS JUST A THIEF IN AURA'S ROOM. I CHASED HIM AWAY.....

IT SEEMS TO ME THAT AURA NEEDS A LOT OF PROTECTING!

5-9

Dale is aroused by the commotion.....
NEXT WEEK
DEADLY INGRATITUDE

FLASH RECOGNIZES ONE OF BARIN'S SERVANTS AS THE SNEAK THIEF WHO HAD PROMISED TO GO STRAIGHT_____

DON'T WORRY, FELLOW__I'LL LET YOU GO AND YOU'RE SAFE, AS LONG AS YOU STAY HONEST__WHAT'S YOUR NAME?

GROMBO, SIRE__THANK YOU FOR YOUR KINDNESS__I WON'T FORGET IT, SIRE__

IT WAS THE MOST THRILLING THING BARIN, DEAR___A THIEF IN MY ROOM LAST NIGHT____FLASH ALMOST CAUGHT HIM!

HE MUST BE FOUND!

IT WAS NOTHING, AURA_____FORGET IT..

PERHAPS, DARLING, SHE DOES NOT WANT TO FORGET IT_____

GROMBO, TREACHEROUS HIMSELF, CANNOT BELIEVE THAT ANYONE ELSE WILL PLAY FAIR_____

I CAN'T TAKE ANY CHANCES

BUT FROM WHERE DALE SITS, SHE CAN SEE INTO THE PANTRY__

FLASH__THAT WAITER PUT SOMETHING IN YOUR FOOD!

SO YOU WON'T DRINK THIS SOUP, YOURSELF, EH? YOU RAT! YOU TRIED TO POISON ME!

OH, DON'T KILL ME! HAVE MER-CY__I BEG YOU!

5·16

Copr. 1937, King Features Syndicate, Inc., World rights reserved.

I'LL HAVE THE SCOUNDREL THROWN TO THE GROUND FROM THE HIGHEST TREE__WHY DID HE WANT TO POISON YOU, FLASH?

HE WAS THE SNEAK THIEF___ HE THOUGHT I'D TELL ON HIM, I GUESS___ DON'T KILL HIM, BARIN· PUT HIM IN PRISON

NEXT WEEK:- A CORNERED RAT

GROMBO, THE THIEF WHO TRIED TO KILL FLASH, IS TAKEN TO PRISON----------

GROMBO ANGRILY PROWLS IN HIS CELL-----

FLASH AND DALE FORGET PAST DANGERS AS THEY VIEW BARIN'S KINGDOM------

BARIN SOUNDS THE ALARM AND ISSUES LAST MINUTE INSTRUCTIONS TO HIS OFFICERS

THE SOUND OF MARCHING FEET ECHOES THROUGHOUT THE KINGDOM, AS SCOUTING PATROLS LEAVE IN ALL DIRECTIONS---------

=NEXT WEEK=
THE HUNT

FLASH AND BARIN LEAD THE PURSUIT OF THE TREACHEROUS GROMBO----

THAT FOOT-PRINT BACK THERE MAY HAVE BEEN HIS...

WE MUST CATCH HIM BEFORE HE CAN SEND WORD TO MING!

SUDDENLY, THE BRIDGE, CUT BY THE FUGITIVE, CRASHES....FLASH HURLS BARIN TO SAFETY------

AS HE SLIDES OFF THE BROKEN SECTION OF THE BRIDGE, HE GRABS A LOOSE ROPE AND HANGS ON!

YOU SAVED MY LIFE, FLASH... I DON'T KNOW HOW TO THANK YOU, OLD FRIEND!

DON'T TRY, BARIN... LET'S SEE WHAT WE CAN DO FOR THOSE MEN OVER THERE -- NO HOPE FOR THE POOR FELLOWS WHO FELL... ANOTHER SCORE TO SETTLE WITH GROMBO!

FLASH CUTS A SECTION OF VINE-ROPE FROM THE HAND-RAIL OF THE BRIDGE--HE FASTENS ONE END TO A TREE AND HURLS THE OTHER END TO THE WAITING SOLDIERS-----

...THE SOLDIERS MAKE THEIR END FAST AND SET OUT, HAND-OVER-HAND, FOR THE OPPOSITE SIDE OF THE BROKEN BRIDGE....

5-30

NEXT WEEK = HOT ON THE TRAIL

TRAILING THE TRAITOR, GROMBO, FLASH AND BARIN REACH A SENTRY-POST ON THE TREE HIGHWAY........

IF THIS SENTRY HAS LET OUR MAN SLIP PAST HIM........

HM-M-M.. LOOKS AWFULLY QUIET

POOR FELLOW_THE SENTRY PAID FOR HIS CARELESSNESS WITH HIS LIFE.....

THE BODY'S STILL WARM, FLASH..... GROMBO CAN'T BE FAR AHEAD OF US.. TELL THE DRUMMER TO SEND A MESSAGE FOR THE PATROLS AHEAD TO CLOSE IN.....

THEY'VE FOUND THAT SENTRY_I'VE GOT TO TAKE TO THE TREES....

...BUT THE HUNTED MAN "LISTENS-IN"..

GROMBO IS UNAWARE THAT HIS MOVEMENTS ARE BEING WATCHED BY THE TERROR OF THE FORESTS_THE HORNED APE-MEN OF MONGO!

DON'T KILL ME! I HATE TREE-MEN, TOO! I'LL HELP YOU TO CATCH A LOT OF THEM! THEY'LL FOLLOW ME AND YOU CAN KILL THEM!

UGH! WE TRY IT!

MEANTIME, DALE IS DETERMINED TO FOLLOW FLASH.....

I WARN YOU, IT'S DANGEROUS--WON'T YOU CHANGE YOUR MIND?

I DON'T CARE, CAPTAIN TRUNO.... I HAVE TO BE WITH FLASH....

NEXT WEEK— APE RAIDERS

6-6

CAUGHT BY A TROOP OF HORNED APES, GROMBO PROMISES TO HELP THEM TRAP HIS PURSUERS———

I'LL BE A DECOY... I MEAN, THEY HUNT ME, I RUN..THEY CHASE ME, YOU KILL THEM!

UGH, KILL TREE-MEN!

CAPTAIN, ORDER THE DRUMMER TO STAY HERE AND SUMMON MORE TROOPS..... WE'LL MARK THE TRAIL AS WE GO....

I'LL BET GROMBO JUMPED THERE! SEE, THE BARK IS TORN!

FLASH AND BARIN FIND THE TRAIL.....

A LITTLE LATER....DALE'S PARTY REACHES BARIN'S DRUMMER ----

THEY'RE FOLLOWING GROMBO INTO THE JUNGLE, SIR..IF I MAY SAY SO, IT'S TOO DANGEROUS FOR THE LADY, SIR--

HER MIND IS MADE UP, DRUMMER---- WHICH WAY DID THEIR MAJESTIES GO?

...DEEP IN THE JUNGLE... ONE OF BARIN'S ADVANCE GUARDS GIVES A YELL OF TRIUMPH..ARROWS LEAP FROM HIS LONGBOW.......

GROMBO YELLS IN TERROR, AS THE ARROWS COME UNCOMFORTABLY CLOSE !......

...SUDDENLY, THE TREES RAIN APE-MEN, FROTHING WITH THEIR ANCIENT HATRED OF THE SUPERIOR TREE-MEN!

NEXT WEEK— OUT-NUMBERED

104

UNDER COVER OF DARKNESS FLASH STARTS TO ASCEND THE SWAYING VINE LADDER ⋯⋯⋯

MEANWHILE IN THE LAIR OF THE APE-MEN GROMBO BARGAINS WITH THE BRUTES ⋯⋯

AND OUTSIDE FLASH SIGNALS FOR HIS HANDFUL OF MEN TO START THEIR ATTACK!
NEXT WEEK: AN AMAZING TRICK ⋯⋯⋯⋯

IN ANSWER TO FLASH'S SIGNAL, TRUNO SHOUTS A CHALLENGE TO THE APE-MEN......

COME OUT, YOU COWARDS!

....FLASH'S TRICK LURES THE APE-MEN FROM THEIR TREE-HOUSE....

ONLY THREE! KILL! KILL!

...THEY RUSH DOWN THE LADDER.....

CUT YOUR END, TRUNO!

SUDDENLY, FLASH SPRINGS THE TRAP !.......

THE APE-MEN PLUNGE A THOUSAND FEET TO THEIR DOOM !.........

BARIN! CALL OUT! WHERE ARE YOU?

FLASH ENTERS THE TREE HOUSE TO RESCUE HIS FRIEND, KING BARIN.........

NEXT WEEK ÷ A ONE-MAN SIEGE

FUNNY BARIN DOESN'T ANSWER MY CALL..I DON'T LIKE THE LOOKS OF THIS PLACE.... SOMETHING TELLS ME I'D BETTER WATCH MY STEP.........

FLASH'S STRATEGY GETS HIM INTO THE TREE-HOUSE WHERE BARIN IS BEING HELD CAPTIVE..............

AND IN THE COUNCIL-ROOM WITH THE CAPTURED KING, GROMBO AWAITS FLASH'S COMING.........

THE FOOL DOESN'T REALIZE THAT THE LIGHT IN THE ROOM CAUSES HIS SILHOUETTE TO SHOW THROUGH THE SKIN WALL...... HERE'S WHERE I SURPRISE HIM!

ONE MOVE, GROMBO, AND I'LL RUN YOU THROUGH! DROP THAT SPEAR AND STEP OVER TO THE DOORWAY!

GROMBO'S SPEAR CLATTERS TO THE FLOOR, BUT HE SUDDENLY LUNGES FORWARD..... FLASH'S SWORD RIPS THROUGH THE TOUGH HIDE WALL A SPLIT SECOND TOO LATE!.........

7-18

WHY DIDN'T YOU KILL HIM, FLASH? HE WAS WAITING TO KILL YOU IN COLD BLOOD...GO AFTER HIM, FLASH..NEVER MIND ME! IF HE ESCAPES, HE'LL PUT MING ON YOUR TRAIL!

YOU'RE ALL THAT MATTERS, BARIN...I COULDN'T RUN HIM THROUGH IN COLD BLOOD.... AND I DIDN'T KNOW THERE WAS ANOTHER WAY OUT OF THIS PLACE....

NEXT WEEK
MAROONED

RESCUING BARIN IN THE LAIR OF THE HORNED APE-MEN, FLASH HUNTS FOR THE TRAITOR, GROMBO..........

I'LL SEARCH THIS SIDE AND YOU TAKE THE OTHER ROOMS....

HE CAN'T GET OUT OF THIS HOUSE AND, WITH THE LADDER CUT, NEITHER CAN WE....

....FLASH SIGHTS GROMBO WHO WHIRLS AND LETS FLY WITH A SPEAR WHICH FLASH SKILFULLY DEFLECTS------

...GROMBO BARS THE DOOR TO DELAY PURSUIT, BUT FLASH CHARGES AND BURSTS IT ASUNDER....

....THE WILY TRAITOR SLIPS THROUGH A WINDOW.....

AS SOON AS I HEARD ALL THE NOISE, I CAME ON THE RUN... SO HE GOT AWAY, EH?

PHEW, HE'S A SLIPPERY DEVIL!...BUT HE CAN'T GET AWAY FROM HERE ANY MORE THAN WE CAN!

7-25

FAR BELOW, DALE AND TRUNO WATCH ANXIOUSLY-----

THERE THEY ARE... FLASH AND BARIN WAVING FROM THAT WINDOW! THEY'RE SAFE!

NEXT WEEK

**PERILS OF ESCAPE**

**F**LASH AND BARIN CLIMB OUTSIDE OF THE TREE HOUSE OF THE APE-MEN, GIVING UP THE SEARCH FOR GROMBO--------

WE'RE TOO HIGH FOR TRUNO TO THROW VINE ROPES TO US--WE'LL HAVE TO CLIMB DOWN THE TREE--IT'S A GOOD THING WE FOUND THAT AX

LET ME DOWN SLOWLY, BARIN---YOU'LL HAVE TO HANG ONTO ME 'TIL I CUT THE FIRST TWO OR THREE NOTCHES, THEN YOU CAN FOLLOW AS I CUT THE REST--- YOU'LL BE BEARING MY WEIGHT MOST OF THE TIME, BUT I'LL CUT THE NOTCHES DEEP ENOUGH TO GIVE YOU A GOOD FOOT-HOLD---

DON'T WORRY, FLASH--I'LL HANG ON TOOTH AND NAIL!

I ONLY HOPE BARIN'S IRON MUSCLES HOLD OUT! LUCKY THIS WOOD IS SOFT---

**D**ANGLING AT THE BOTTOM OF THE ROPE WHILE BARIN HOLDS ON TO THE CROTCH OF THE TREE; FLASH CHOPS THE FIRST TWO NOTCHES ------

**S**LOWLY DIGGING FOOTHOLD AFTER FOOTHOLD, FLASH AND BARIN FINALLY REACH THE NEXT BRANCH FAR BELOW THE APE-MEN'S TREE HOUSE ------

BARIN, MY HAT'S OFF TO YOU--- YOU'RE A TOUGH MAN! HI, TRUNO, THROW US A VINE!

8-1

YOU HAVE FLASH TO THANK FOR SAVING THE LIFE OF YOUR KING, TRUNO!

I NEVER THOUGHT I'D SEE YOU ALIVE AGAIN, YOUR MA-JESTY!

HERE, LET ME WIPE AWAY YOUR TEARS-- DON'T CRY, DARLING-- I'M SAFE NOW--

I KNOW IT, SWEETHEART-- THAT'S-- THAT'S WHY I'M CRYING!

NEXT WEEK = **BARIN'S SECRET ORDER**